LONDON'S
RIVERSIDE PUBS

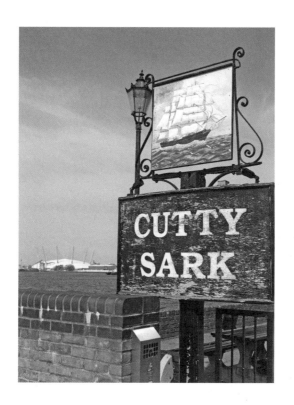

LONDON'S RIVERSIDE PUBS

Tim Hampson

Read. Learn. Do What You Love.

Published 2016—IMM Lifestyle Books
www.IMMLifestyleBooks.com

IMM Lifestyle Books are distributed in the UK by Grantham Book Service,
Trent Road, Grantham, Lincolnshire, NG31 7XQ.

In North America, IMM Lifestyle Books are distributed by Fox Chapel Publishing,
1970 Broad Street, East Petersburg, PA 17520,
www.FoxChapelPublishing.com.

ISBN 978 1 5048 0021 1

10 9 8 7 6 5 4 3 2 1

Printed in Singapore

CONTENTS

INTRODUCTION

This book is a journey, a tour from the greenery and gentle English countryside of Walton-on-Thames to the point where the River Thames almost meets the open sea. It is an expedition that embraces the fresh water of the Thames above Teddington and its locks, marking the river's transition into a salty conduit that once brought the wealth of the world to the wharfs and docks that lined the riverside. The Thames and the other waterways which course through London are liquid history.

Royal connections

Walton-on-Thames is on the very western edge of London, a former Saxon settlement from where a river journey eastwards takes travellers past Hampton Court, built by Cardinal Wolsey from 1514 to 1521 but later aquired by Henry VIII. Its gardens are famous for their formal grandeur while the palace has a renaissance ceiling said to be one of the most perfect in the country. Then on to Kingston, once famed for its fisheries. The river was fordable here in Anglo-Saxon and Roman times, which probably bought wealth to the area. Its importance was cemented in medieval times when it was first bridged.

In Richmond little remains of a palace built by Edward I in the thirteenth century and subsequently enlarged by Henry VII. Here, the slopes on the banks give many fine views of the Thames and the bridge that was built in 1777. Two of England's greatest painters, Turner and Reynolds, came to paint the beautiful scenes.

A further royal influence is found at Richmond Park that was created to provide a hunting ground for Charles I. Today it is one of London's greatest parks, both a playground and home to a huge variety of wildlife, especially large herds of deer. It's well worth making a detour to the top of Richmond Hill from where you can see the centre of London.

From Twickenham, east

Twickenham is another former Anglo-Saxon settlement, though today it is probably best known as the home of rugby union in England. Near the bridge is the original foundation of Syon, a monastery founded by Henry V to pay for the sins of his father. It was later moved to its current site. Syon House is now the home of the Duke and Duchess of Northumberland, and the gardens were designed by Capability Brown. Look across the river and you'll see the world-famous Kew Gardens, which has more than 25,000 plants. One of its most popular atractions is the Xstrata Treetop Walkway, which lets visitors wander through the tree canopy to see the gardens from a completely new perspective. There is also an underground Rhizotron display, showing how plants' roots work.

From Kew the river then begins its journey through the centre of the capital, passing the Houses of Parliament and the Tower of London. The Houses of Parliament, or the Palace of Westminster as it is also known, date from the time of Edward the Confessor. It was a royal residence until the time of Henry VIII but was virtually

destroyed by fire in 1834, and only Westminster Hall and St Stephen's Chapel survive complete. It was rebuilt in the neo-gothic style in 1840. The Commons Chamber, where Members of Parliament debate, was destroyed by German bombs in 1941 and it was completely rebuilt and opened in 1950.

The skyline here is dominated by Big Ben, which is not the name of the Palace of Westminster's clock tower but its giant bell. The chime is broadcast before the start of many news programmes, which first happened on New Year's Eve 1931. Close by you'll see the London Eye, a relatively new addition to London's skyline. At 135m (443ft), it's the tallest cantilevered observation wheel in the world, rising high above the buildings. Known as the 'Millennium Wheel' when it was opened in 2000, it is now one of the UK's most popular tourist attractions. On a clear day it provides views for more than 40km (25 miles) in any direction. The giant wheel was intended to be an allegory for the end of the twentieth century, showing time turning from one century to the next.

The Millenium footbridge to London Bridge

Further down river, just past Blackfriars Railway Bridge, is London's newest bridge – the Millennium footbridge – that links Bankside with the City. It opened on 10 June 2000 but was quickly closed two days later. People on a charity walk felt the bridge sway and it was quickly nicknamed the 'Wobbly Bridge'. It remained closed for two years until engineers managed to solve the problem. The bridge offers a clear view of the south side of St Paul's Cathedral, framed by the bridge supports, and some of the sweeping and soaring spires of Sir Christopher Wren's other churches. A scene from the Harry Potter film *The Half-Blood Prince* was shot here.

St Paul's is one of London's most iconic and poignant images. A Christian church was certainly here in 604, and there might have been a Roman temple before that. A stone church was built in 675

but it was destroyed by the Vikings and rebuilt in 962, and that was in turn destroyed by fire more than 100 years later. The next church was completed in 1220 but it fell into misuse and was often used as a stables and by market traders. In 1634 Inigo Jones was commissioned to restore it, but his work was thwarted by the Great Fire of London in 1666. In 1675 work began on Wren's new grand design, and this was finally completed in 1710 when the final block of Portland stone was put in place by Wren's son. Restoration work in the 1930s, which saw the strengthening of the dome, probably saved it from destruction during World War II when bombs destroyed the high altar.

London Bridge was always falling down – well, so the nursery rhyme says – but the bridge's latest incarnation, which opened in 1973 with its flying, sweeping design by Harold King, looks secure enough. No one knows when the first bridge was built here, but certainly by Roman times there was one. Destroyed and rebuilt many times, a stone bridge was built in 1176. It later became a street across the Thames with shops, houses and a chapel but eventually they fell into disrepair or sank into the London clay. This bridge lasted until 1825 and it's here that London originally began. This is where the Romans, with their elephants, settled in AD43.

Londinium and the frost fairs

The Romans called the place Londinium, though they retained the ancient Celtic name for the river, Tamesis. The emperor Claudius clearly realized the strategic importance of the site. The rise and fall of the tide meant that the invaders' boats, carrying cargo, soldiers and much more, could travel many miles inland. And while the marshy land was not ideal for building, it did give access to many parts of England and remained the only place in London where you could cross the river by bridge, certainly until 1750.

A mini-ice age engulfed the northern hemisphere from the fifteenth century, causing the Thames to freeze on many occasions, creating havoc for maritime trade. However, from the seventeenth century the freezing created a new form of entertainment, the frost fair. Londoners, ever willing to make a profit from any situation, organized stalls on the ice, selling freshly cooked food or souvenirs while jugglers and clowns entertained large crowds. The frost fair of 1813–14 was the last because Europe was warming up and a new bridge, built some 10 years later, had much wider arches, improving the flow of water. And when the Victorians harnessed new technology, installing locks and building the great docks, much of the flow of the Thames came under human control. The river has never frozen since.

The Tower to the Thames barrier

Journeying east, look north and you'll see the Tower of London's White Tower, built by William the Conqueror as a garrison and armoury to keep him safe from the people he had invaded. It has since been a royal palace, a zoo and was once the home of the Royal Mint. It was also a prison until 1820 where the kings of Scotland, France and England, Lady Jane Grey, Sir Thomas Moore, Sir Walter Raleigh and even the future Queen Elizabeth I languished (for six months in the case of the young princess) or were beheaded. The entrance to the tower from the river is known as Traitor's Gate and through its portal many a sad soul took their last

steps. The nearby impressive Tower Bridge, which opened in 1894, is a steel structure with neo-gothic towers made of stone. Its two 1,000-ton bascules still regularly open to let river craft pass beneath.

By the beginning of the eighteenth century, London was the largest city in Europe and the home port for the expanding British Empire. The river was so busy at this time that Daniel Defoe estimated that there were about '2,000 sail of all sorts not reckoning barges, lighters or pleasure boats or yachts' using the wharves and quays that are the start of London Docks. St Katherine's docks are to the east of the Tower, and from the bridge down to Tilbury there were once five great systems: London & St Katherine, India and Millwall, Royal Victoria & Albert, King George V and, on the south side, the Surrey Commercial. In their heyday each dock would have specialized in particular goods. At Limehouse a lock gives access to Regent's Canal and the Lee Navigation, the journey's end for most inland craft.

Downstream the river passes the revitalized docklands in the Isle of Dogs area with huge offices where there were once wharfs and cranes. On the south side stands the grandeur of Greenwich, with the Old Royal Naval College one of the river's most fabulous landmarks. The glorious eighteenth-century building was designed to house old and disabled seamen on the site of a former Tudor palace, a favourite residence of Henry VIII and the birth place of Elizabeth I. Inside the Royal Naval College is the spectacular Painted Hall, now used as a dining room, with paintings by Sir James Thornhill that took 19 years to complete. This is where the body of Lord Horatio Nelson lay in state after his death at the Battle of Trafalgar in 1805.

Finally, on to the Thames Barrier that was built in the 1980s to stop rising tides from flooding London. The first line of defence against a surging North Sea, the Thames Barrier was officially opened in 1984. So far it has done its job well, protecting London from the powering tidal Thames but, if the battle is won, the war is not. London is built on clay and is slowly sinking into it. One day a new and even more powerful redoubt will have to be built.

The many faces of the Thames

It is not hard to imagine the Thames with one of its many cloaks on. The river has seen Celts, Angles and Saxons living alongside it. The Thames is the tranquil, magical and sometimes chaotic world of *Three Men in a Boat* and *The Wind in the Willows*. The Thames was the world's greatest port. The Thames saw the scavenging mudlark and thieving footpad (two obsolete words, the first meaning someone who scours the river mud for anything of value, the second a robber). The Thames is where Samuel Pepys watched the flames engulf much of the city during the Great Fire of London. There is the Thames of industry and sweating stevedores (or dock labourers). And there is the Thames where, in 1790, William Wordsworth composed a poem from Richmond Bridge, called 'Lines written near Richmond, upon the Thames at Evening'. He wrote,

'Glide gently, thus for ever glide, O Thames! that other bards may see'. In 1819 Joseph Turner painted a panorama of the Thames, entitled 'Richmond Hill, on the Prince Regent's Birthday'.

Perhaps one of the most potent images is of the Thames as a royal river. Elizabeth I was born in Greenwich, imprisoned in the Tower, she reigned at Whitehall and died at Richmond. The Thames was wider then and the water purer. Salmon and swans would watch the spectacular state barges travel up to Hampton Court or even Walton Court or down the river past the glories of Greenwich.

Alehouses, inns and taverns

The River Thames is the UK's second longest river and the longest in England. It stretches for 345km (215 miles) from its trickling source in the Cotswold Hills to the tumultuous open sea. From Walton-on-Thames eastwards there are 34 bridges, almost one for every mile to the Thames Barrier with many pubs en route. And it is beer that should be enjoyed in these pubs.

Nothing remains of the places where early Londinium residents drank beer. By the medieval period the streets of London would have had many alehouses, which looked little different from the surrounding houses where the householder – often a woman known as a 'brewster' – served home-brewed ale and beer. Some might have even offered accommodation, often no more than bedding on the floor or in a barn, perhaps sharing with horses.

Inns were purpose-built buildings for travellers and, since old London was a busy port and a place for pilgrims, the inns would have been packed. There was a large number around London Bridge, many of the inns being owned by the powerful monasteries. One – the now demolished Tabard, which was south of the river – was where the writer Geoffrey Chaucer sent off his travellers on the road to Canterbury in 1380.

Besides the alehouses and inns there were taverns but, since they sold wine, which was then expensive, there weren't that many. However,

some were built with galleries around a courtyard to provide an area for plays. One good example is the George, a short walk from the south side of London Bridge, off Borough High Street, Southwark, which still has some of its galleries intact. (Details of this pub are not in this book but they can found in *London's Best Pubs*.) All three kinds of drinking house advertised their business with a sign outside the premises. A pole above the door, garlanded with foliage, signified an alehouse. From the fourteenth century, inns and taverns hung out a pictorial sign by which they could be identified in an illiterate age. In the sixteenth century many alehouses did the same. The tradition has continued to this day for licensed premises, since they were exempt from the Georgian restrictions on hanging signs. Many of the earliest signs used images drawn from heraldry, but by Georgian times there was greater variety reflecting trades, political affiliations and even events on the other side of the world.

From opulence to disrepair and success

By the mid-eighteenth century larger alehouses in London were becoming widespead, while inns beside the major roads or wharfs grew in grandeur with new ones being created to meet the needs of those now travelling by coach. (During this period the alehouse began to be known as a public house.) From the start of the nineteenth century the practice of building purpose-built pubs took hold and, as the population grew, so did the number of pubs. The late Victorian era also saw the creation of ostentatious interiors, notable for their opulently decorated mirrors, tiled walls and etched glass. And the development of the canals saw many pubs built to provide both drink and food for their new clientele. Furthermore, the development of the railways meant that pubs were now built in places, such as Hampton Court, to attract the day trippers.

However, the twentieth century saw many London pubs fall into disuse or disrepair because of the Great Depression, the two world wars and the fact that the city was no longer a thriving port. Furthermore, after 1945 there were government restrictions on building materials, with housing taking priority. But by the 1970s pubs were making a comeback. Old favourites were restored, new ones were built, people became more affluent and started eating out in pubs while women became more economically and socially independent and wanted pubs to suit their tastes. In addition, the riverside and the docks were redeveloped and had brand new pubs while old buildings, which might once have been a warehouse or bank, were converted into glittering glass palaces where people could enjoy themselves. The very best pubs were entering a new era of success.

Brewing beer

The Thames, as we know it today, was created 10,000 years ago, formed as the ice that had covered most of the UK melted away. People have

lived along the Thames Valley since prehistoric days, 6,000 years ago, and it seems likely that these early settlers who were attracted by the fertile ground turned from hunter-gatherers into farmers. They grew grain to feed themselves and their animals, and also started to make and consume a mysterious drink that made them feel good – beer. The ingredients couldn't be simpler: cereal (normally barley), water and yeast; today hops are added, but there is plenty of evidence that other plants and herbs were once used to inject flavour and/or keep the beer from spoiling. We know that barley, an essential ingredient of most beers, was grown 5,000 years ago and a British coin from about the first century BC has an ear of cultivated barley on one side. Ale, like bread, was an essential part of everyone's diet.

It is likely that once the Romans left London, alehouses sprang up next to London Bridge and along the main roads. An alehouse was probably no more than a simple hut with a branch from an evergreen bush hung outside on a pole to attract customers. Later, with the arrival of William the

Conqueror, the population around London Bridge grew and so did the practice of brewing beer. In fact by 1437 brewing in London had grown to such an extent that a charter was granted to brewers in the city of London to form their own trade association, the Brewers' Company.

By the sixteenth century there were great beer houses close to St Katharine's dock near Tower Bridge, with beer also being exported overseas to the Low Countries to be consumed by British troops. But it was in the Reformation, when a large number of Flemish immigrants settled in Kent bringing with them the practice of growing hops, that the traditional way of making beer was challenged. There was a huge row about the efficacy of using hops in beer, but from then on the practice was adopted.

London's brewers

As London grew as a great trade centre, so brewing increased. In the early part of the sixteenth century there were 26 large brewers in the city, though most beer drunk here was still made by publican brewers. By the seventeenth century the City of London had more than 400 taverns, with names that were still commonplace 200 years later, brewing by the Thames or close to it. Courage, Whitbread and Charrington were on the river or had their own wharfs, and became part of the growing capitalist, industrialized society that saw London brewers send their beer across the globe. It wasn't uncommon for admirals to send urgent requests to

London brewers, complaining that the brewers in towns like Newcastle couldn't supply enough beer to meet the demand.

In the fourteenth century the farmers of England looked to London as the market for their grain or hops, and accordingly great warehouses were built. Barley from Hertfordshire came by boat down the River Lea while craft brought the hops up the Thames from Kent. Beer production was now on a massive scale to slake the thirst of the 700,000 people living in the London area. Beer was a vital source of carbohydrate and, because it had been boiled, it was safer to drink than water.

New competition

The area around London Bridge became an important brewing centre. The soft water extracted from London's wells was particularly good for the brewing of darker beers, such as milds and porters. The trade grew and London (with a population of more than three million in the 1870s) was, without doubt, the greatest brewing centre in the world. However, as tastes changed and transport became easier because of the canals and railways, people started to drink the lighter-coloured ales and bitters brewed in Burton upon Trent and Yarmouth. London's brewers started to lose their pre-eminence and at railway stations such as St Pancras giant vaults were built to store the barrels of beer coming from the Midlands.

Throughout the latter half of the twentieth century London's brewers were gripped by merger mania, and many were bought by brewers from other parts of the country and later from overseas. This, combined with the rapid rise in property prices and the fact that roads replaced rivers and canals as the main means of transporting goods, meant that the City of London was no longer a brewing centre. By 2010 all but one – Fuller Smith & Turner – of the many brewers operating in Victorian London had gone.

However, brewing in the capital is not dead, and a new breed of smaller brewers now exists. London is home to some of the country's most creative brewers, as more than 60 have opened in the last few years. And where better than a pub on the River Thames or on one of London's other waterside locations to have a drink?

London's waterways have seen war and peace, and today they face an optimistic future with major new developments taking place on the shore. New parks are being built and, where there was once industrial pollution, fish swim again and kingfishers and herons dive. Fishermen, joggers, cyclists and families out for an afternoon stroll are all now able to enjoy the riverside paths while commuters, on fast-moving modern clippers, can rush up from the industrial grandeur of the Thames Barrier to the towering triumph of the London Eye. The Thames is alive and well, and where better to go for a good beer, lively company and the sound of lapping water.

Cheers
Tim Hampson

Where to go if you like...

FRESHWATER THAMES

On its journey from Walton to Kingston, the Thames begins to change. The gentle lowland river, which rose in the Cotswolds, begins to transform, gathering energy and power. The water meadows and pastures with native grasses and herbs are left behind. Buildings come closer to the banks and the gentle rural landscape gradually becomes more urban. In ancient times this part of the Thames Valley was ideal for settlements: the fresh water and fertile land encouraged fishing and the cultivation of crops and livestock. 'The time has come', wrote Lewis Carroll, 'to talk of many things of shoes and ships and sealing wax – of cabbages and kings'. The Thames has seen it all.

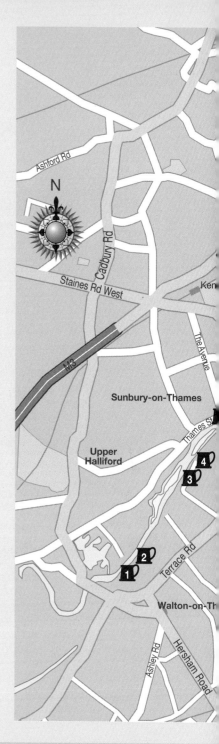

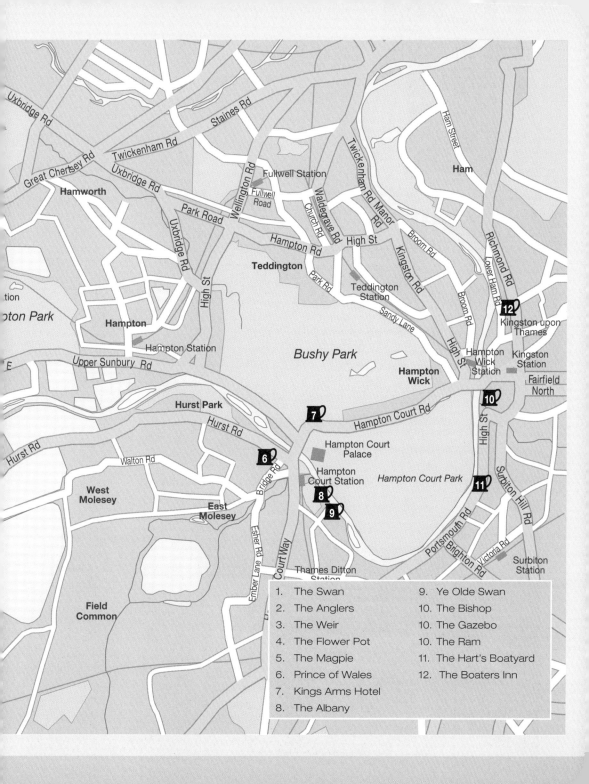

1. The Swan
2. The Anglers
3. The Weir
4. The Flower Pot
5. The Magpie
6. Prince of Wales
7. Kings Arms Hotel
8. The Albany
9. Ye Olde Swan
10. The Bishop
10. The Gazebo
10. The Ram
11. The Hart's Boatyard
12. The Boaters Inn

The Swan

50 Manor Road, Walton-on-Thames, Surrey, KT12 2PF

BEERS: Wells and Young's range

The Swan's spacious and well-manicured garden sloping gently towards the water is the perfect place to watch the river world go by

The large, smart garden of the Swan sweeps down to the riverside where swans, ducks and pigeons wait in hope for tit bits. It is a perfect place to relax while watching the leisure boats pass by. Inside there are large, elegant modern rooms decorated in dark wood. There are several high comfortable chairs and tables, and plenty of space for drinkers to stand by the bar. There are wooden floors throughout. One room is decorated with large imposing photographs of swans. The lighting is subdued but with a hint of warm elegance, and a smart gas-fired wall-feature flickers by the entrance.

A pub has probably been here since 1770, when it appeared on the Walter Leigh Manorial maps and was then just a small alehouse. The present building dates from the late 1890s or possibly a little later, and the pub gets its name from the ancient ceremony of swan-upping performed each July on the Thames. All the swans are carefully caught,

counted and marked on the bill, and are then divided between the Crown and companies of the Dyers and Vintners. The uppers still stop at the Swan on their way up to Staines from Walton.

The songwriter Jerome Kern met his wife here. In 1910 he visited the pub while on a boating trip on the Thames. Apparently he immediately fell for Eva Leale, the daughter of the licensee, and they married in Walton. A copy of the marriage certificate is on display in the pub. Perhaps Kern was inspired by the river to write 'Ol Man River'? Kern went on to write 'Smoke Gets in your Eyes', the hit musicals *Showboat* and *Sally*, and the films *Swing Time* and *Covergirl*.

Wells and Young's excellent range of ales are sold, and Young's Bitter is used in the pub's wholesome steak and ale pies and beer-battered fish. Sausages made with Young's Special Bitter are also served. If you fancy another pub, the small but perfectly-formed, 500-year-old Manor Inn is down the road.

The Anglers

Riverside Road, Walton-on-Thames, Surrey, KT12 4PE

BEERS: Marston's range

The Anglers with its smart riverside seating and air of comfortable luxury will soon have passing walkers and cyclists hooked by its location

At times the river seems impossibly busy, crowded with barges, pleasure boats and rowing boats. The Anglers is a wonderful place to watch the craft go by. In the 1890s, when Jerome K. Jerome was researching his novel *Three Men in a Boat*, the Anglers was still a collection of wooden huts with a boathouse next door, which is now an art gallery. It became a pub in 1910, and has been modernized and refurbished several times over the years. Drinkers can sit on the riverside patio or in the spacious ground floor bar where there's a large log fire. Upstairs there is a restaurant with great views.

There's a contemporary menu and fresh food sourced from local suppliers. All the meat is supplied by Walton's favourite butcher, the Taste of Walton, and dishes include wholesome burgers with chunky chips, pork belly and venison. The organic bread is freshly baked on a daily basis and is made with organic flour from Shipton Mill, in Gloucestershire, suppliers to Prince Charles' Highgrove Estate.

The pub serves Marston's range of ales including Pedigree. In its heyday Pedigree was regarded as the most sublime and complex of British ales. It is the classic Burton pale ale and has a hint of caramel, followed by a gush of malty, spicy Fuggles and Golding hops with their fresh apple taste. Brewed with the uncompromising hard waters from Burton upon Trent, the beer has a nutty delicateness that can be masked by the sulphurous 'snatch' from the sulphates in the area's legendary brewing water. The brewery still uses the classic union system to ferment the beer. Housed in high-ceilinged maturation rooms, the system was introduced in

the 1840s and was once widely used for the production of 'better' ales. After fermentation begins, the beer is transferred into 264 linked oak barrels; the production of carbon dioxide, as a by-product of fermentation, helps expel the yeast from the beer through swan-necked pipes into collection troughs. Brewing scientists regarded the system as unparalleled for the production of bright, clean, strong-tasting pale ales.

The Weir

Waterside Drive, Walton-on-Thames, Surrey, KT12 2JB

BEERS: Fuller's London Pride, Brakspear Bitter, Old Speckled Hen

There is something comforting, even old-fashioned, about the inside of this well-loved pub and its riverside garden – it is a real treasure

Dashing kingfishers, startled coots and serenely floating swans are frequently seen on this stretch of the river, but parakeets? They've adopted parks and gardens in this leafy London suburb, which comes as a surprise if you think they live only in southern Asia. It is not uncommon to see the birds by the riverside. In fact escaped parakeets have been nesting in Surrey since the nineteenth century, but the population remained very low up to the 1960s when it started to grow and, by the mid-1990s, it really took off. One theory is that they escaped from the set of *The African Queen,* filmed in Ealing, West London, in 1951. Another is that a pair released by rock musician Jimi Hendrix in Carnaby Street, central London, in the 1960s may be partly to blame. However, the mild waters in recent years have certainly helped the birds prosper.

There is something old-fashioned about this pub, which is on the riverside at the end of a lane behind the Walton-on-Thames leisure centre. The inside suggests a lost Edwardian elegance, despite the presence of a large flat TV screen. A large coal fire provides comfort on cooler days. The décor is dark, warm and comfortable. The walls are adorned with brassware and copper. Shining frying plans vie for wall space with bellows, spoons and old prints. The food is homely and wholesome, with lamb shank a favourite.

The garden is frequented by the many walkers and cyclists who use the attractive riverside walk. The gates of Hampton Court Palace are only 5km (3 miles) away, down river. Outside the pub, there are terraces with welcoming chairs and tables where drinkers can sup pints of English ale – often from local brewers – while listening to the water tumbling and rushing over the weir. A good time to visit is during one of the pub's beer festivals on the first bank holiday of May or at the end of August. There is a separate garden area for those over 21. The pub is often at its best on a summer's day as the sun begins to set.

The Flower Pot

Thames Street, Sunbury-on-Thames, Surrey, TW16 6AA

BEERS: various

A former coaching inn, The Flower Pot is a perfect blend of the old and the new. Perfect for a special meal. It serves good beer too

The pub's name is a useful guide to the age of the pub. It was adopted in the seventeenth century when Oliver Cromwell came to power. The Puritans disliked names that referred to religious imagery, and it is likely that the pub originally had a sign containing lilies, the emblem of the Virgin Mary. Such pubs changed their names, putting the emphasis on the container rather than its contents.

The exterior of this smart pub is just what you'd expect of an eighteenth-century coaching inn on the way to London, but inside it has been transformed and today it is smart, open-planned, light and trendy. There are nice pieces of artwork on the walls and two large tropical fish tanks. Some might think it more of a restaurant than a pub, but there is a good, changing list of various cask ales, which often include beers from Fuller's, Wells & Young's, St Austell and Brakspear, and drinkers can choose to stand at the modern central bar or sit at one of the tables. The menu is English and modern. The pub stands on a corner on the way into town, across the road from the Thames, which it is possible to see from the Flower Pot's small terrace.

The town is home to Sunbury Millennium Embroidery, in the Millennium Embroidery Gallery, which is within the Walled Garden next to Sunbury Park. The pub's hotel rooms make it an ideal base for anyone wanting to explore the area further, especially Kempton Park races, Kew Gardens and Hampton Court Palace. Each July, Lower Sunbury sees the start of the Swan Upping ceremony, when two livery companies begin their annual count of the swans on the upper reaches of the Thames. It is sometimes hard to imagine that such a pretty little town can only be 25km (16 miles) from the clamour and bustle of central London.

The Magpie

64 Thames Street, Sunbury-on-Thames, Surrey, TW16 6AF

BEERS: Greene King range

The Magpie is a gem and its terrace is the perfect place for river watching and daydreaming about the delights of river cruising

Set close to the road, it is difficult to see the full grandeur of the entrance to the Magpie. Downstairs, an often busy bar leads onto a small, attractive riverside terrace where you can drink pints of Abbot Ale and dream of owning one of the pleasure boats in the boatyard opposite. Those wanting more of an intimate conversation can use the book-lined sitting room. Upstairs there's a room with even more prominent views of the river. On sunny days the Magpie is very popular, but on cold winter days you'll probably only find the locals.

A friendly pub, it has close links with the London Irish Football Club but it's probably best known because it was right here, in 1889, that the Grand Order of Water Rats – the oldest theatrical charity and brotherhood – was established. A plaque outside, unveiled in 1939 by the inspirational ventriloquist Fred Russell, who was King of the Water Rats in 1903, 1914, 1929 and 1939, records the organization's jubilee year. One of the founder members of the charity, Joe Elvin, was given a small trotting pony named Magpie by impresario Joe Thornton. Together they formed a syndicate and agreed to give the pony's winnings to charity to support hard-up actors.

They didn't know what to call the charity. One syndicate member suggested the Noble Order of the Star, but no, too posh he was told. Then, on a trip to Epsom races on a rainy day, with the pony pulling a cart with the actors inside, a bus driver shouted at the soaking group, 'What's that'? 'That's Magpie, our trotting pony,' said Joe. 'Looks more like a bloody water rat', said the driver. Hence the name.

The comedian and fellow founder Wal Pink said that the rat was the most unloved creature of all, and that they'd make it respected. He said, 'If you turn the word rats backwards the word star is revealed. We'll elevate the lowest to the highest; a rat is a vole and vole is an anagram of love, and that's what we'll be, a brotherhood of love'.

Prince of Wales

23 Bridge Road, East Molesey, Surrey, KT8 9EU

BEERS: Greene King range

People have been flocking to the Prince of Wales for more than 150 years – the pub exterior is a fine example of Victorian pub design

The pub probably couldn't have been built in any other era than the 1850s. Its gaunt gothic style and elaborate gables belie a swaggering pride in progress. Victorian East Molesey prospered because of the railway that came to the village in 1849. The railway brought people and wealth to the area, as many flocked for a day out in Hampton Court Palace, which opened to the public in 1838. Within a short time several other pubs also opened close to the palace, providing refreshments for the crowds who came for a day out. The pub was initially called the Railway Hotel, but it was later changed to its current name as a tribute to the oldest son of Queen Victoria. Many pubs of this era were so named.

Inside, the ground floor has seen many guises over the years and there are few remnants of its Victorian heritage. Today it's modern and contemporary with a light and airy feel. Currently, sausages feature on the menu, and what could

better than a plate of sausage and mash with a pint of bitter? Old Speckled Hen is a wonderfully warm-flavoured beer bursting with body. Malt-loaf and toffee flavours combine with a satisfying bitterness on the back of the tongue. The beer was first brewed in 1979 to celebrate the fiftieth anniversary of the MG car factory in Oxfordshire.

The beer was named after an old Featherweight Fabric Saloon car that was used as the MG factory runabout. The workers parked the car outside the paint shop where it would normally get splattered in paint, and it became known as the Owld Speckl'd Un. This became Old Speckled Hen when the beer was launched. The beer was brewed by Morlands in Abingdon, but both the brewery and the MG factory are long closed and the beer is now brewed in Bury St Edmunds by Greene King. Its creator, the now retired brewer Bill Mellor, says it still tastes as good as ever.

Kings Arms Hotel

Lion Gate, Hampton Court Road, East Molesey, Surrey, KT8 9DD

BEERS: Hall & Woodhouse

The Kings Arms has as much style and class as the adjacent Hampton Court – its luxurious bedrooms are ideal for an overnight stay

The Georgians knew how to design buildings with elegance and the Kings Arms, situated by the Lions Gate entrance to Hampton Court and its world-famous maze, oozes classical style. The exterior has the confident and robust symmetry one expects from a building of this era, and inside it is a mix of dark timbers and tastefully exposed brickwork and some marvellous stained glass. The main bar has an exquisite floor mosaic with the pub's name inscribed. It was built by Italian craftsmen more than 300 years ago, who were then working at the palace. The pub also has nine highly individual and luxurious en-suite bedrooms, each with a different Henry VIII theme.

Opposite the pub is Bushy Park, the second largest of the Royal Parks that covers more than 1,100 acres. It has its own distinct rural character and is famed for the Christopher Wren-designed Arethusa Diana Fountain that forms the centrepiece to the equally famous Chestnut Avenue. Parts of the area where the park now is were inhabited during the Bronze Age more than 4,000 years ago, and there is also clear evidence of medieval field boundaries. During World War II General Dwight D. Eisenhower planned the D-Day landings from his headquarter at Camp Griffiss in the park. Today the park is famed for its wildlife, especially the herds of fallow and red deer, and it is also reputed to be the place where the modern game of field hockey was developed.

The ales served at the Kings Arms come from the Hall & Woodhouse brewery in Blandford Forum, Dorset. The brewery, which has a heritage almost as old as Hampton Court, was founded in 1777 and is still owned by members of the original families. In the mid-1980s Hall & Woodhouse wanted to produce a new beer. A number of test brews were prepared using water drawn from the Dorset chalk aquifer 50m (165ft) below the brewery and yeast that was first used in the brewery in 1934. One brew stood out from the others, but what to call it? After several glasses in the sampling room the head brewer, the redoubtable John Woodhouse, struggled to his feet – and fell over. Tanglefoot was born and you can drink it right here at the Kings Arms.

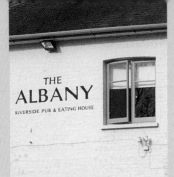

The Albany

Queens Rd, Thames Ditton, Surrey, KT7 0QY

BEERS: changing list of cask beers and lagers.

A bustling, modern, stylish pub with more than a touch of class – it is just outside Thames Ditton and over the river from Hampton Court

Do not miss the stylish Albany, which stands on the riverbank opposite Hampton Court Palace and its fine riverside walks. Named after the Lord Darnley who married Mary Queen of Scots, mother of James I, the Albany dates back to 1886 and, for some years, music-hall acts sang and danced here, including the legendary Marie Lloyd. In 1996, after a refurbishment, it was briefly called the Fox on the River but it has now reverted to its original name.

On busy days space can be at a premium, inside and outside this stylish bar and restaurant, with its mixture of comfy sofas, cane and wood tables and chairs, but somehow everyone fits in. The food is English with a continental twist and many dishes are specially meant for sharing.

Incidentally, if you're interested in visiting Hampton Court Palace, a ferry boat often runs between the two banks. In the sixteenth century the palace was the home of Cardinal Wolsey, a favourite of Henry VIII, who took it over when Wolsey fell from grace. In the seventeenth century William III began a project at Hampton Court that he believed would surpass the grandeur of the Palace of Versailles. His vision was never finished but, today, the palace with its harmonious clash of Tudor and Baroque architecture is a popular tourist attraction. And if you like fisherman's stories, note the tale of the Reverend George Harvest, one of Thames Ditton's most famous scions, who died in 1780, a man of legendary forgetfulness. A keen fisherman, he whiled hours away in pursuit of gudgeon, a small carp-like, freshwater fish. But his love of the hook, line and sinker caused much trouble on his wedding day. Betrothed to the Bishop of London's daughter, he decided on a spot of fishing before taking his wedding vows. The lure of the fish was too much for him and he missed his wedding and, unsurprisingly, the jilted lady promptly called it off.

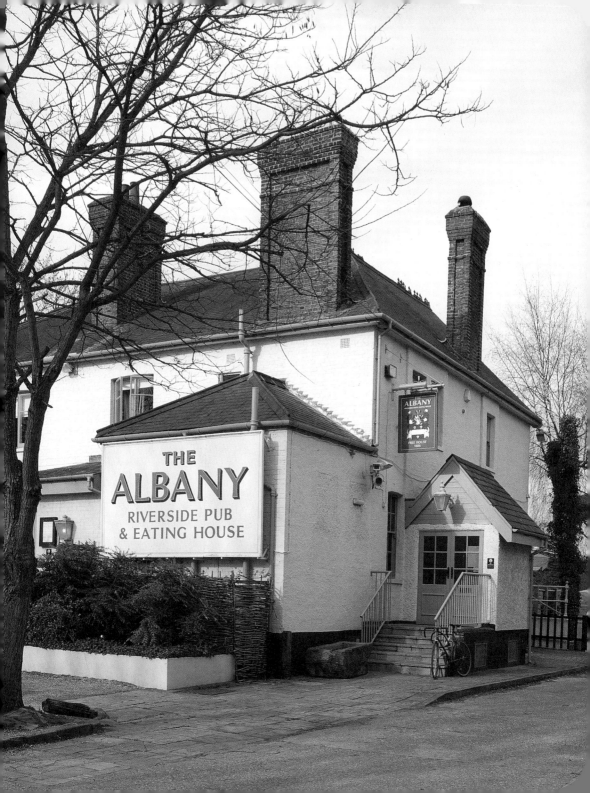

Ye Olde Swan

Summer Road, Thames Ditton, Surrey, KT7 0QQ

BEERS: Greene King

Full of nooks and crannies of the thirteenth century, Ye Olde Swan is a delightful collection of well-worn rooms

This rambling black and white pub has recently been given a much needed refurbishment, which has enhanced its well-worn charm and elegance. An attractive Grade I listed building, this thirteenth-century inn has its own 25m (80ft) long jetty where customers can moor a boat under the watchful eyes of others sitting on the large patio. In Victorian times large sailing barges from the Port of London would moor here to load or unload cargo, when the pub was often used by sailing crews and waggoners.

Next to the pub is a smart, gated, suspension footbridge built in 1939, which takes pedestrians to Thames Ditton Island. The island, one of three and the largest on this stretch of the river, is 350m (1,150ft) long and has 47 houses and a population of around 100. Henry VIII was a frequent visitor, and his seal of approval for the inn is displayed in the British Museum. In fact the king was a frequent traveller on the river, moving between his London palace and his summer home, Hampton Court. To make his arrival and departure easier and grander, a section of river (then narrower and more bendy) was dug out, creating the islands. Before locks were built on the river in the eighteenth century, it was tidal right up to Sunbury, meaning that much of the area, including the islands, was subject to flooding at high tide. Even now, many of the houses are built on stilts just in case there's a flood. In the 1900s holiday chalets were built on the islands for the people of Kingston. As well as providing access for the island's residents, the bridge is used to bring in water, electricity and gas and take out the sewage. There are no cars on the island.

The Bishop

2 Bishops Hall, Kingston-upon-Thames, Surrey, KT1 1PY

BEERS: Wells & Young's

The pub's fine terrace and spacious bars offer excellent riverside views – meaning it can get very busy as soon as the sun starts to shine

The pub was built in 1979 on the site of an old tannery, which was once a thriving industry in Kingston, and proves that good pubs do not always have to be in old buildings.

It was named by a Young & Co shareholder after the brewery's chairman, the ebullient John Young, had requested names for the new pub at the company's AGM. The company's AGMs were famed for the volume of beer that was drunk and the lavish food. The chairman (always known by staff as Mr John) would often wear a costume, such as boxing gloves or a beekeeper's hat, to emphasize a specific point. Sadly the AGMs were scaled down when, after one particularly good lunch, some shareholders 'slightly the worse for wear' were found leaving the building with some of the silver service in their pockets.

The pub's name refers to the Bishop's Palace, built on the riverside here for William of Wykeham (1320-1407). A multi-talented man, he was amongst other things Bishop of Winchester, founder of New College in Oxford and Winchester College, and he helped build part of nearby Windsor Castle. The pub itself offers unbelievable views of the Thames, the downstairs bars is light and airy, the upstairs River Room is the perfect place to enjoy supper and, as it gets dark, to enjoy the lighting on Kingston Bridge. Outside there is a fine terrace and a renovated walkway up to the bridge, which is perfect for watching the scullers, like hyperactive mayflies, scooting along the river.

Kingston was important because, until a wooden bridge was built in Putney in 1729, it was the first crossing point on the Thames upstream from London Bridge. Early bridges were made of wood, and certainly existed from the thirteenth century. The foundations for the current bridge were laid in 1828. For more than 650 years a toll was charged for crossing the bridge, but to the pleasure of citizens this 'crossing tax' was abandoned in 1870. They celebrated with a firework party, which ended with the burning of the toll gates.

The Gazebo

Thames Street, Kingston-upon-Thames, Surrey, KT1 1PH

BEERS: Samuel Smith

The Gazebo is a good place to relax after visiting the nearby shops – its comfy sofas upstairs are particularly sought after

Kingston-upon-Thames is a mecca for people who like pubs, with three riverside venues close together – the Bishop, the Ram and the Gazebo. The latter stands right on the riverside and splits into two levels. There's a modern but traditional downstairs bar with large patio doors that open on to the riverside and a more chic upstairs where drinkers can stretch out on comfy sofas, or sit on the terrace and enjoy the sunshine.

The beers are supplied by Samuel Smith, an enigmatic, innovative but secretive brewer in Tadcaster, North Yorkshire. Unusually, in this era of brand images, the brewery rarely brands its pubs, has removed its logo from the drays and has the reputation for always selling beer at lower prices than its rivals! Samuel Smith's Old Brewery Pale Ale is a sublime example of a strong English bitter. A traditional Yorkshire-style bitter, it has a dark tan colour and the effervescence helps form a brimming white head on top. There's a malty taste with a hint of butterscotch, nuts, fruit and spicy hops. It has the crisp, clear taste one expects from a beer fermented in Yorkshire Squares. The grist of pale and crystal malts is boiled in traditional mash tuns (a vessel in which malt is boiled to release fermentable sugars) and the hops are Goldings and Fuggles, added late to inject a dash of spice. The yeast has been used at the brewery for more than 100 years, and its vigour and vitality creates the rich, foaming head in the fermenting room.

On busy days the Gazebo and the surrounding area are also full of vigour and vitality. There are almost 5km (3 miles) of one of the most attractive stretches of the River Thames with walks and cycle routes to Hampton Court, Teddington and Richmond. North of Kingston Bridge is Canbury Gardens, a leafy spacious park and the perfect place for a picnic, fishing or just feeding the ducks.

The Ram

34 High Street, Kingston-upon-Thames, Surrey, KT1 1HL

BEERS: Greene King range, plus guests

Less grand than Kingston's other riverside pubs, The Ram offers a warm welcome and a choice of fine beers

Dubbed Kingston's friendliest pub, the Ram has recently had a needed makeover, which has enhanced its personality. The pub has become something of a beer paradise and offers more than 20 bottled beers and 17 others on draught from its tap room. The regular meet-the-brewer evenings, where brewers come along with samples and are happy to share their knowledge, are popular with customers.

Note the long, narrow, paved garden that runs down to the riverside but, given its prime location on this attractive stretch of the Thames – heading from Kingston towards Surbiton on one side and Hampton Court on the other – seats are at a premium on busy days. A moment's walk away is Kingston's ancient, Market Place, next to the Old Town Hall. A pleasant place to wander, people listen to buskers and look round the market that's open six days a week with its many stalls selling local produce and foods from around the world. There's also an annual German Christmas market where glüwein and bratwurst can be bought.

The Ram is also close to the Rose Theatre, making it a useful place to meet before and after a play. Opened in 2008, the design of the auditorium took its inspiration from the Elizabethan Rose Theatre, once situated on London's Bankside and demolished in 1606. It has the same shaped stage, with a semi-circular seating and pit area, where audiences can sit on cushions to watch performances. One of the most unusual nearby sights is in Old London Road, Kingston, close to the station. 'Out of Order', or 'Tumbling Telephones' as it is sometimes called, is a sculpture by the Scottish artist David Mach. It was commissioned in 1988 as part of the landscaping for a road improvement scheme, and consists of 12 old red telephone kiosks leaning against one another, like a row of falling dominoes.

The Hart's Boatyard

Portsmouth Road, Surbiton, Surrey, KT6 4HL

BEERS: good range of real ale

Modern and stylish, The Hart's Boatyard is a fine example of breathing new life into a building which had formerly fallen into disrepair

Hart's was once a boatyard but, in recent years, it has been transformed into a quirky, intriguing pub, split into three levels with decking over the water, making it a perfect place to watch the sun set over Hampton Court Palace. Often there is a ferry taking people across to the other side of the river.

The décor is softly lit, chic and comfortable with big sofas, chunky chairs, solid tables and open fires. The menu is international and modern with some homely favourites. Shared dishes are a favourite, being particularly popular with students from Kingston University, and often small groups will share a Spanish tapas of stuffed pequillo pepper, a baked Camembert with rustic bread or a Greek mezze. Unusually for a pub so near the centre of Kingston, it has a large car park that makes it a favourite for visiting parents wanting to treat their starving undergraduate children. There is a good, changing list of English ales, and the pub has Cask Marque accreditation, a pub industry measure of good quality.

Outside, there are rowers, swans and moorhens on the river. Next door is the Thames Sailing Club, founded in 1870, and the first river sailing club in the country. The club is home to Thames A Raters, large three-handed dinghies with 14m (45ft) high masts, designed to catch the wind above the trees that line the river. Built for river racing, they still compete in regattas that start and finish just outside. The oldest wooden-hulled boat still competing was built in 1902.

The stories of Kingston and the Thames are closely entwined. Seven Saxon kings of England were crowned here, and the name, Kingston, is derived from Cyningestun, which means royal estate or palace. In the Middle Ages the town was an important inland port, used for ferrying goods to London, and it was renowned throughout England for the quality of its salmon fisheries. Salmon is on the menu at Hart's Boatyard, though it is no longer caught locally.

The Boaters Inn

Lower Ham Road, Kingston-upon-Thames, Surrey, KT2 5AU

BEERS: range of cask ales

A beer lover's paradise. The Boaters Inn deserves its reputation for keeping cask ales well. It is also a jazz venue

You need your walking legs if you arrive at Kingston by train because Boaters is a good 15 minutes stroll from the station. Situated in Canbury Garden, it is a large, open-plan, friendly pub with its own mooring on the bank of the Thames. It is a welcome find for any riverside explorer as this part of the river doesn't have many watering holes.

The garden is Victorian in origin, and home to the Kingston Rowing Club and Sigi Cornish Tennis Club. It also hosts Kingston's annual Green Fair. The site was a location for the 1973 episode of *Doctor Who*, the 'Invasion of the Dinosaurs'. The Time Lord's Tardis, which stands for Time and Relative Dimension in Space, materializes in a deserted park. All Gallifreyan Time Lords used a Tardis to travel between dimensions, but a fault in the Doctor's machine means that its external look is stuck in 1963 earth time, which is why it always appears as a police box (where the police could make emergency calls before the invention of walkie-talkies and mobile phones). The exact landing site is close to the tennis courts.

The Boaters is family-friendly and the food home-made. On sunny days its outdoor area soon fills and drinkers spill into the gardens. But even having to use plastic glasses doesn't dampen customers' enthusiasm for the range of cask ales on sale. On Sundays jazz bands play and, while its reputation is yet to rival the splendid Bull at Barnes, its fame is growing for the quality of the music and for TEA, an English ale brewed by the Hogs Back Brewery in Tongham, Surrey. A copper-coloured beer, it is full of malt and hop fruit flavours, well rounded and delightfully drinkable.

TEDDINGTON
TO PUTNEY

The lock complex at Teddington marks the start of the Thames as a tidal river. The watery corridor becomes wider and offers a variety of habitats for a wide range of wildlife. Down to Richmond the river still has an air of a rural corridor along which people from another age could travel with ease, using the river like a motorway. But, as the river gets wider, so the modern buildings to the sides get bigger and closer together. The countryside is now far behind and London can now be clearly seen. Today, part of this stretch of the river is used for one of world's greatest river races, the annual clash between Oxford and Cambridge Universities.

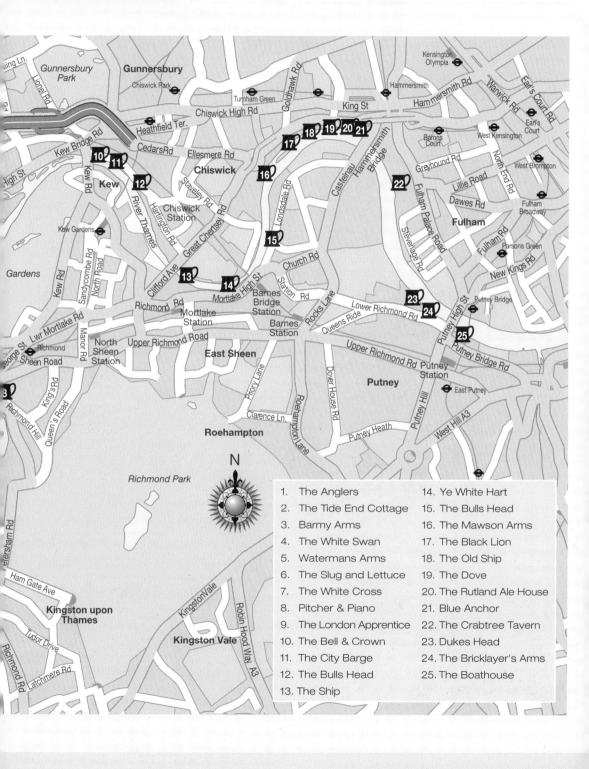

1. The Anglers
2. The Tide End Cottage
3. Barmy Arms
4. The White Swan
5. Watermans Arms
6. The Slug and Lettuce
7. The White Cross
8. Pitcher & Piano
9. The London Apprentice
10. The Bell & Crown
11. The City Barge
12. The Bulls Head
13. The Ship
14. Ye White Hart
15. The Bulls Head
16. The Mawson Arms
17. The Black Lion
18. The Old Ship
19. The Dove
20. The Rutland Ale House
21. Blue Anchor
22. The Crabtree Tavern
23. Dukes Head
24. The Bricklayer's Arms
25. The Boathouse

The Anglers

3 Broom Road, Teddington, Middlesex, TW11 9NR

BEERS: Fuller's range

An excellent pub with a large and spacious garden, it is ideal for families wanting to while away a sunny afternoon

Close to Teddington Lock, the location of the famous Monty Python fish-slapping dance, the Anglers (founded in 1795) is a perfect place for river watchers. Its situation makes it very popular, especially with families because children can enjoy the play area. A large pub, people can sit inside or relax outside in the garden. It features a barbecue, hog roasts, coffee shop and moorings, and serves Fuller's London Pride. Pubs of this size and location can occasionally seem overwhelmed by their success but not so here, and it is a marvellous place to while away an afternoon and enjoy the fine location.

The actor, impresario and composer Noel Coward is one of Teddington's most famous sons. Born in 1899 he was renowned for his wit and turn of phrase. From an early age he was an incredibly successful actor and playwright, and in the 1930s he had four plays on simultaneously in London's West End. During World War II he abandoned the stage and joined the war effort, working for British intelligence in Paris. But the then prime minister, Winston Churchill, had other ideas. He wanted Coward to entertain the troops. 'Go and sing to them when the guns are firing – that's your job', he told him. And so Coward toured the theatres of war across Europe, Asia and Africa, even visiting America. He wrote and recorded many war-themed popular songs, including 'London Pride', and wrote the immortal line 'mad dogs and Englishmen go out in the midday sun'.

The Tide End Cottage

8-10 Ferry Road, Teddington, Middlesex, TW11 9NN

BEERS: Greene King

A small locals' pub with plenty of heart that welcomes visitors to this part of the river. The Tide End Cottage is beloved by many fishermen

The Tide End Cottage is a small, comfortable, friendly pub, full of river and fishing memorabilia, probably built around 1820. There is a small terrace out the front and a conservatory at the back. It is very much a locals' pub. Close by is Teddington Studios. The first productions were made here in the era of silent films more than 100 years ago, and the studios were based in the gardens of Weir House. But it was in the 1960s that the studios came to prominence, not making films but television programmes such as *The Avengers*, starring Patrick Macnee, Ian Hendry and Honor Blackman, and *The Benny Hill Show*, which was made for more than 20 years from 1969. Other entertainment programmes included *This Is Your Life*, *The Des O'Connor Show*, *Opportunity Knocks* and *Thank Your Lucky Stars*. Perhaps the likes of Bruce Forsyth, Tommy Cooper and Morecambe and Wise nipped in for a pint?

Teddington is one of the most significant spots on the Thames and is where the freshwater river of *The Wind in the Willows* and *Three Men in a Boat* meets the ebbs and flows of the tidal Thames – a world divided by three locks. From The Tide End Cottage to the North Sea, the river twists and turns 25 times before it pours out into the open sea, more than 100km (62 miles) away. There's freshwater until Battersea, when salt gains superiority. Before the locks were built in about 1810 the river was tidal as far as Staines.

Barmy Arms

The Embankment, Twickenham, Middlesex, TW1 3DU

BEERS: changing list of cask ales

Its great riverside location means the beer garden is a really nice place to spend a warm afternoon or evening – it is well used by rugby fans

Many might ponder why the pub is called Barmy, and like all the best legends no one really knows. Perhaps the pub used to brew beer, in which case the word 'barmy' might refer to the froth that forms at the top of a fermenting vessel. Others say a one-time landlord was somewhat empty headed; for a time the pub's sign did indeed hang upside down and the mens and ladies signs on the pub's toilets were transposed.

It is hard to imagine that this quiet riverside pub – quiet, that is, unless a Six Nations rugby tournament is on – with its quintessential, genteel English leafy aspect, stands opposite one of the most famous rock-music locations in the world. Opposite is Eel Pie Island, a very early venue for two of the world's greatest and most influential rock-and-roll bands,

The Rolling Stones and The Who. The Eel Pie Hotel and Eel Pie Island Jazz Club hosted most of the 'greats' of the Swinging Sixties, including Rod Stewart and Eric Clapton.

The Eel Pie Hotel dated back to the nineteenth century when it was frequented by Charles Dickens and, until 1957, when a footbridge was built, it could only reached by ferry. Then a Kingston junk shop owner, Arthur Chisnall, had the idea of opening a jazz club there. However, the brashness of rhythm and blues, and rock, brushed jazz aside and many of the country's up-and-coming rock and blues stars, including John Mayall's Bluesbreakers, the Moody Blues and the Yardbirds, all carried their equipment over the bridge to the hotel. The hotel fell into disrepair and burnt down in 1971.

The White Swan

Riverside, Twickenham, Middlesex TW1 3DN

BEERS: wide range of cask beers

The White Swan is famed in the world of rugby for its hospitality but it offers something for everyone, especially if they like a party

Rugby is not just part of the White Swan, it *is* the White Swan. Around the wall of the L-shaped bar are all kinds of rugby artefacts, including club shirts, trophies, ties, pictures and balls. On Six Nations or other international match days it is certainly worth the scrum to try and get in here. The pub even sponsors its own rugby team, the Bulldogs. The pub also has its own golf society, holds legendary New Year's Eve parties and hosts a raft race in July. Once the pub was the haunt of rock stars playing over on Eel Pie Island, but on match days you'll get a big dose of 'Swing Low, Sweet Chariot'. The other big attraction is food. There's a help-yourself buffet laid out in summer on a large table and a barbecue on the patio. Winter brings out solid traditional fare and terrific Sunday roasts.

The nearby Flood Lane hints at why this picturesque riverside pub, which has been on this site since 1690, has an elevated position on the north bank of the Thames. Across the narrow road there is a small riverside garden, which often floods when the river runs high.

Watermans Arms

10-12 Water Lane, Richmond, Surrey, TW9 1TJ

BEERS: Wells & Young's range

A friendly pub which still retains much of its Victorian charm, but its menu of Thai food reflects today's tastes

One of the oldest pubs in Richmond, Watermans Arms was originally called the 'King's Head at the Ferry in Richmond' and it dates back at least to 1660. It stands in a cobbled street that runs up from the river to the post office. The pub oozes character and charm, and still retains its Victorian two-bar layout.

The fashion for breaking pubs into different rooms reached its peaks in the 1890s, when pubs much larger than Watermans would be split into many rooms being named the 'parlour', the 'private' and 'public bar', 'tap-room', 'ladies' room' and 'snug'. Certainly, most pubs would have been split into two, with a public and a saloon bar for labourers and white-collar workers respectively. There might also have been a small space for selling jug and bottled beer for people who wanted to drink at home. Traditionally the public bar would have been more sparsely decorated than the saloon, and the beer would have been sold a few pence cheaper than in the saloon. If the pub sold food it might have been served only in the saloon bar.

The pub's menu is best described as traditional with an Asian twist. Reflecting the changing nature of the British palate, the menu contains many Thai dishes, such as a Thai red or green curry. Directors Bitter, first brewed by Courage, is often on sale. A classic English ale, it is robust enough to compliment spicy food. The beer has a distinctive rich fruity flavour with the dry overtones of hops. Apparently it was originally brewed exclusively for the directors of the brewery who eventually decided to sell it commercially.

The Slug and Lettuce

Water Lane, Richmond, Surrey TW9 1TJ

BEERS: Marston's Pedigree, Ringwood forty-niner, changing list of guest ales

A bustling modern bar, which is part of a national chain. It is the perfect place for lunch, dinner or even breakfast

With stunning views of the river and a large seating area outside, it is easy to understand the popularity of this pub. Often just called the Slug, it is part of a large nationwide chain of bars, all with the same name, many found in busy town centres. This pub is particularly popular with groups looking for a good night out and special food offers. Opening early in the day, people also pop in for breakfast. It has a modern, upbeat interior with a variety of comfortable seating and some interesting works of art. In the 1830s the building housed Collins Brewery, one of London's many breweries. Today, cocktails are very popular and there is a comprehensive range of lagers and popular European beers, such as Hoegaarden, available on draught.

Nearby is the largest royal park in London, Richmond, which from its highest point has an uninterrupted view of St Paul's Cathedral, 20km (12 miles) away. The park is London's largest Site of Special Scientific Interest, and is also a National Nature Reserve and Special Area of Conservation, renowned for its grazing herds of red and fallow deer. Also look out for the rare stag beetle, Britain's largest native ground-dwelling beetle that can fly. Adult females can be up to 5cm (2in) long and some males may reach 7cm (2.7in). In addition at least another 1,000 species of beetle live in the park, which thrive among the collection of ancient trees, including a large number of oaks.

The White Cross

Water Lane, Richmond, Surrey, TW9 1TH

BEERS: Wells & Young's

One of the most popular pubs on this stretch of the river, offering some fantastic views. Its range of cask ales make it a perfect choice

If the river is rising, don't park in front of the pub as flooding is a problem for any building that fronts the Thames. Too many unfortunate motorists have ignored this cardinal rule. Indeed, a sign by one of the pub's doors says 'entrance at high tide', a reminder of the challenges of riverside life.

This distinguished pub on Richmond's waterfront dates from the 1830s with the top floor being added just before World War I. Inside, a stained-glass panel reminds customers that it stands on the site of a former convent of the Observant Friars, whose insignia was a white cross. The order was founded in 1499 by Henry VII, and the friars were a branch of the Franciscan order, instituted about 1400 by St Bernardine of Sienna. The friars were renowned for their zeal in bringing sinners back to God. All went well until Henry wanted a divorce from Catherine of Aragon. The friars protested against his divorce and marriage to Anne Boleyn. Indeed, their voices were some of the loudest to oppose the king. They paid a deadly price – some were executed, others died in prison and the convent, with the others in the order, was ransacked.

The White Cross, with large windows and stupendous riverside views, is a warm, friendly place though at times it can be extremely busy. One curiosity is the fireplace situated beneath a window. On summer days the patio is crowded.

Pitcher & Piano

11 Bridge Street, Richmond, Surrey, TW9 1TQ

BEERS: Brakspears, plus four changing regional ales

After exploring Richmond's historic streets and fine shops the pub's attractive terrace is the perfect place to relax with a beer or cocktail

The terrace of the Pitcher and Piano has to be one of the best places to relax with a drink. The trade magazine *Theme* voted the pub's riverside situation as one of the top 20 world-wide locations to enjoy a summer drink.

The pub is one of a chain of bars all with the same name, the first being opened in Fulham in 1986, to much acclaim, by the brewer Marston's. With white walls, wooden floorboards and halogen lighting all becoming popular in people's homes, these pubs were designed to replicate the look. Built inside a building with a Georgian façade, the interior of the Richmond Pitcher and Piano is a combination of traditional hard-surfaced mahogany floors with modern wooden tables and sleek chairs.

At weekends the pub often has DJs, and sporting events are shown on large plasma screens.

Richmond, with its collection of winding, cobbled streets, is a particularly fine place to explore on foot. Richmond Bridge was opened in 1777, replacing a ferry that was operated by the Crown. There were two boats, one for people and one for horses and small carts. Heavier vehicles had to go up river to Kingston. It is the oldest bridge still standing over the Thames in the Greater London area. The area's name derives from the time of Henry VII, who built a Tudor palace here; he named it Richmond after his favourite Yorkshire earldom. Mary Tudor used it frequently and Elizabeth I died there, but during the Civil War it fell into decay.

The London Apprentice

62 Church Street, Isleworth, Middlesex, TW7 6BG

BEERS: wide range of real ales

A large and friendly pub that is well used by locals as well as those out walking and cycling along the riverside

Where does the pub get its name? There was once a popular ballad – 'The Honour of an Apprentice in London' – that told the story of the adventures of an apprentice who, like Richard the Lionheart, 'robbed a lion of his heart'. After 'his matchless manhood and brave adventure in Turkey', he married the king's daughter. Well, maybe. In any event the pub dates back to Tudor times when the apprentices of the London livery companies rowed out to Isleworth during their free time and sang the song.

The pub was rebuilt during the first half of the eighteenth century. The first recorded licence dates back to 1731 and, until 1739, it was kept open all night for the benefit of river travellers. Famous visitors included Henry VIII, Charles I, Charles II with his mistress Nell Gwynne, Lady Jane Grey and Oliver Cromwell, all of whom had close links with nearby Syon House. Open throughout the spring and summer, the gardens at Syon (landscaped by Capability Brown in the mid-eighteenth century) are renowned for their extensive collection of rare trees and plants.

The pub now has a smart walled riverside terrace with views of Kew Gardens on the other side of the river, a comfortable downstairs bar, and upstairs there is a Regency-style room with a river view. You can still see some fine historical features, including a mural panel recording a bell ringing competition in 1848 when five bell ringers completed a peal of 5,093 changes of 'Grandsire Caters' in a record 3 hours 20 minutes, and a pair of plaster ceiling reliefs over 300 years old. A tunnel from The London Apprentice apparently ran 300m (985ft) to the port of Old Isleworth and is believed to have been used by smugglers to pass their contraband, under the eyes of excise officers, to the cellars of the inn. The pub also has an etched window with the decorative lettering 'Isleworth Ales'. It is a reminder of the time when London had many local brewers. The company was registered in 1886, taken over by Watney Combe Reid in 1924 and closed soon after the end of World War II.

The Bell & Crown

11 Thames Road, Chiswick, W4 3PL

BEERS: Fuller's range

Several pubs can be found on this attractive part of the river, this pub is a favourite for anyone who enjoys Fuller's beers

Chiswick is known for many things – linoleum was invented here, the first Royal Navy torpedo boat was built here and it's the home of Cherry Blossom boot polish – but it also has some excellent pubs along the river. It is sometimes difficult to imagine that the centre of London and the noisy Great West Road are so close.

The pub was first licensed as the Bell & Crown around 1787, although it probably had an earlier name. It was probably built to take advantage of a newly constructed bridge over the river. The west London brewer Fuller, Smith & Turner bought it in 1814 and rebuilt it 1907. The pub expanded to its current size in the 1980s when two adjoining shops were bought and the large conservatory added. A friendly place, it is a family-centred pub for locals that welcomes visitors to its quiz and music nights. It is especially enjoyed by those just wanting to watch the river from the patio.

Pubs with the name Bell & Crown often signify allegiance to the monarchy and ringing bells on royal occasions. However, the interpretation of a pub's name is far from an exact science, and sometimes the image does not match the words. Chiswick was once a renowned fishing port and the local church is named after St Nicholas, the patron saint of sailors and fisherman. The Bell & Crown's sign shows two fisherman smugglers, creeping along the riverbank trying to avoid paying tax on imported goods. Legend has it that the pub's cellar was frequently used to store contraband.

Chiswick was the country home of the great painter, engraver and satirist William Hogarth from 1749 until his death. Hogarth's house, on the Great West Road, which has recently been refurbished after a fire, provided a quiet summer retreat from the bustle of city life around his main residence and studio in what is now Leicester Square.

The City Barge

27 Strand-on-the-Green, Chiswick, W4 3PH

BEERS: wide range of cask ales

The pub was almost destroyed by enemy bombing during World War II but today it thrives once more

Known by locals as the Barge, a pub has been on this site since at least 1484 when it was called the Navigation Arms. Queen Elizabeth I gave the pub a 500-year royal charter. It became the City Barge around 1787, the name deriving from the Lord's Mayor's state barge that was moored nearby over winter. In 1940 the pub was virtually destroyed by a German parachute bomb but was rebuilt in the 1950s. However, given the lack of building materials at the time, the work was undertaken using rather plain bricks. The old bar is probably all that remains of the original pub.

A short walk from Kew Bridge, the pub and the towpath outside has featured in two Beatles films, *Help* and *A Hard Day's Night*. In *Help*, Ringo finds himself the sacrificial target of a cult and The Fab Four are chased by a marching band of bagpipers playing

'Scotland the Brave' into the pub. Ringo falls into a cellar, is rescued and everyone ends up singing Beethoven's 'Ode to Joy'. As the pub doesn't have a cellar, that scene must have been filmed elsewhere.

Inside, the pub has two bars – the top and the old bar – though on summer evenings drinkers spill out onto the towpath. The pub is decorated with lots of brass and has a comfortable, quaint atmosphere. This part of the river is home to several rowing clubs, and rowers and scullers frequently pass by. After the end of their training sessions they will often come in for a pint. As a testament to the power of Father Thames, there's a watertight front door, just like a ship's bulkhead, which has to be tightly shut if the river is about to flood.

The Bulls Head

15 Strand-on-the-Green, Chiswick, W4 3PQ

BEERS: wide range of cask beers

With low ceilings and creaking floors this is a perfect pub for anyone wanting to chill out after an energetic stroll along the riverside

For a Puritan, Oliver Cromwell seems to have spent a lot of time in pubs. A sign on the outside wall of The Bulls Head says Cromwell was a frequent visitor here because his sister, the Countess of Fauconberg, lived nearby. However, one day, so the unlikely story goes, he was betrayed to Royalist troops but managed to escape through a tunnel to an island on the river known as Oliver's Eyot. But the tunnel has never been found, and the countess was his daughter not his sister, and she didn't move to Chiswick until after his death!

As for The Bulls Head, it's a near-perfect riverside pub, set amidst the luxurious glamour of multi-million-pound riverside homes. It has expanded –

two cottages on the pub's right were incorporated in 1972 – and is now an apparently disconnected collection of rooms, with the parts being more impressive than the whole. It has creaking floors, low ceilings, open beams and is a pleasant place to relax and enjoy the river. The current menu offers modern pub grub, battered fish and chips, burgers, and steak and ale pies. The pub has Cask Marque accreditation, a pub industry measure of quality, which means that its wide range of cask ales is inspected twice yearly by someone with one of the most enviable jobs in the world, a professional beer taster who has to ensure the beer is served properly.

The Ship

10 Thames Bank, Mortlake, SW14 7QR

BEERS: Fuller's London Pride plus a changing list of guest ales.

The oldest pub in Mortlake, on Boat Race days the embankment outside is packed with spectators watching the finish

On Boat Race days the Ship is a noisy, raucous and fantastically enjoyable place because it stands close by the race's finish at Chiswick Bridge. There's a traditional pub atmosphere with families finding plenty of space, and dogs are welcome. The food is good and it is a great place for barbecues in summer. All the colour and noise is in complete contrast to the adjacent, grandiose Stag Brewery.

It dates from 1487 when it was attached to a monastery and brewed for the local abbot and his monks. Commercial brewing had certainly begun here by 1765, when two different companies brewed on the site. But the two became one and the business prospered, buying both The Ship and the nearby Bull. However, the army made the brewery's fame and fortune because it won a contract to supply beer to British troops in India and the Crimea. On Mortlake High Street it is still possible to see the sign of the 'Mortlake Brewery 1869'. The company was bought by the Watney family in 1898 and the name changed to Watney, Combe, Reid and Co. It is the Watney link that makes older real-ale drinkers scoff. Watney was the first British brewer to make pasteurized beer, known as keg, in the 1930s with Red Barrel. In the 1960s it re-named the beer as Red, lowered its strength and aimed it at students. The beer was a failure and led to the creation of the Campaign for Real Ale, which fought against the growing use of pasteurization and the commoditization of beer.

Today, be it cask or keg, it is not uncommon to find beers from some of London's exciting new wave of breweries on the bar. It is one of the most picturesque spots on the river to enjoy a pint.

Ye White Hart

Terrace Riverside, Barnes, SW13 0NR

BEERS: Wells & Young's range

Rebuilt in the grand Victorian style over three storeys, the pub has commanding views of the river

On Boat Race day the floors of this three-storied pub seem to shake right down to its riverbank foundations as drinkers cheer on the light or dark blues. Situated close to the race's finishing line by Chiswick Bridge, you might well see a finish as close and tight as the bubbles on the head of a pint of Young's Special. Outside there are plenty of benches and tables, normally more than enough to take the overspill from the balconies. Other drinkers sit on the riverbank, but beware the rising tide. The menu offers modern fusion food from the Pacific Rim as well as traditional English pies and roasts.

The White Hart is the oldest pub in Barnes, dating back to 1662, and its terrace is part of the older Tudor roads in the area. The original name was the King's Arms but the pub changed its name around 1776. Originally pubs were called the White Hart to show loyalty to Richard II. The earliest pub to use this heraldic symbol as a name was probably the White Hart in Spalding, Lincolnshire. However, by the late eighteenth century the name had almost become synonymous with a tavern and was widely used to denote a good pub. From 1863 to 1878 the pub here was used for Masonic meetings held by the Rose of Denmark Lodge.

The pub was extensively rebuilt at the beginning of last century, when the balconies were added and it acquired a grand Edwardian affectation. Over the years the grandeur faded, but a recent makeover has brought back its former glory with a modern twist.

The Bulls Head

373 Lonsdale Road, Barnes, SW13 9PY

BEERS: Wells & Young's

The Bulls Head has a worldwide reputation for the jazz concerts which have taken place here since 1959

Somewhat confusingly for the people who lived in the village of Barnes in the seventeenth century, two of its three pubs were called the King's Head – the other became the White Hart – and this one, which has traded since 1672, became the Bulls Head by 1748.

A valuation note for the pub in 1857 notes that the Bulls Head 'tho large and commodious hardly affords a living in the winter scarcely doing any trade'. Business declined even further when the river ceased to be used to transport goods. The pub stagnated for many years. But for the last 60 years it has been the home of jazz, seven days a week, where you can also linger over a pint of Young's sumptuous Bitter, a marvellous amber beer with its overlays of citrus and fresh-bread flavours from the hops and malt.

In 1959 the pub was run by Albert Tolley, a modern jazz fan, who decided to bring bands to this somewhat humble and down-at-heel pub in south London. Some of the world's jazz greats have played here, including Dick Morrissey, Ben Webster, Maynard Ferguson, Humphrey Lyttelton and Ronnie Scott. To celebrate the recent fiftieth anniversary of jazz at the Bull, a concert featured octogenarian Vic Ash, who was the headline act for the first gig and opening night of the club back in 1959. But you don't have to be a jazz fan to come here. Once the pub made a thriving living as a stop for stage coaches. It offered food and refreshment to the horses and travellers. The carriages may have long gone, but the former stables are now a Thai restaurant called Nuay's.

The Mawson Arms

110 Chiswick Lane South, Chiswick, W4 2QA

BEERS: Fuller's

Once a private house, it now serves as the tap for Fuller Smith & Turner's Griffin brewery, and is frequently used by the brewery's staff

The Mawson Arms is linked to Fuller Smith & Turner, one of England's most important real-ale brewers and the only brewer to have won the Campaign for Real Ale's Champion Beer of Britain five times, with three different beers.

Situated by one of London's busiest junctions, brewing has taken place on the site of the Griffin Brewery in Chiswick, south-west London, close to the banks of the River Thames, for more than 350 years. The pub is an ideal place to have a beer before going on a tour of the brewery. The latter's first CAMRA Champion Beer of Britain winner, Extra Special Bitter, was launched in 1971, though it was first brewed in 1969 as a seasonal drink called Winter Beer, replacing Old Burton Ale. A strong, highly complex beer, it is brewed from pale ale and crystal malts and a heady cocktail of Target, Challenger, Northdown and Goldings hops, producing a strong, rich, mouth-warming taste for the winter months. However, it quickly became established as a bottled beer available all year. Fuller's other CAMRA winners are Chiswick Bitter and London Pride, creating a record unmatched by any other brewer.

As an experiment, Fuller's current brewer John Keeling has been storing ESB and their other beers in wooden whisky casks to produce luxurious, smoky, peaty flavours. Since 1997 the company has annually produced a limited edition bottle-conditioned beer – Vintage Ale – that can be kept for many years. They are always brewed with different malt and hops. Bottles of Vintage Ale can be bought from the brewery's shop, next door to the pub. Incidentally, in the US, Extra Special Bitter has come to denote a class of beers that are high in alcohol and full of hop flavours, but without the assertive hop character of an India Pale Ale. Apparently many of America's craft brewers were inspired to make beer because of Fuller's ESB.

The Black Lion

2 South Black Lion Lane, Hammersmith, W6 9TJ

BEERS: Caledonian Deuchars IPA, Fuller's London Pride and St Austell Tribute

The Black Lion is a modern British pub, which is the perfect place to take a break if strolling along the Thames

This pub literally embraces the spirit of Chiswick, as it is close to the home of artisanal Sipsmith Distillery. According to legend, wherever gin was sold it was served with gingerbread. And when the Thames froze over, you could be sure to find a few tents selling hot gin and gingerbread. It was also supposed to be the drink and snack of choice for people watching public executions.

Well, the Thames doesn't freeze over anymore and public executions don't happen anymore, but the staff here will happily sell you a gin cocktail.

This is a country pub close to the city's centre, and has a fabulous frontage on the river's north bank. It has some great beers, good food and a fine garden. It also has a skittle alley, one of the quintessential English pub games, and a resident ghost. It hosts a farmers' market every Saturday.

The Old Ship

25 Upper Mall, Hammersmith, W6 9TD

BEERS: Wells & Young's

A nautical theme runs throughout this historic pub, which is renowned for its full English breakfast and the quality of its cask ales

The Old Ship looks like a large sumptuous summerhouse on the north side of the river, just down from Hammersmith Bridge. A historic pub, it was first recorded in 1722. Always popular, its terrace and balcony quickly fills with people wanting to watch the river and chat. The interior is smart with a maritime theme. There are rope chandeliers, brown leather sofas, a large clock, riverscape paintings and even a boat hanging from the ceiling.

The pub opens at 8am for breakfast and its menu firmly makes it a gastropub. There is the obligatory full English breakfast, Eggs Benedict and Eggs Florentine. Later, boards are written up offering the likes of charcuterie, Best of British or Mediterranean. The main courses include pies, lamb shank and fish and chips. On Sundays there is a popular selection of roasts. There is normally a choice of three cask beers from the Wells & Young's range. Poker is a popular pastime and there's a competition every Tuesday evening.

The nearby Riverside studios where TV programmes, such as *Doctor Who*, were once made is being redeveloped and is becoming an exciting space for art and theatre.

The Dove

19 Upper Mall, Hammersmith, W6 9TA

BEERS: Fuller's range

Time seems to have stood still at this seventeenth-century pub which has to be the most charming on this stretch of the river

The Dove might be the international symbol of peace but it was far from peaceful in June 2009 when a devastating blaze ripped through this seventeenth-century riverside gem close to Hammersmith Bridge. The fire is believed to have started in the first-floor kitchen after a gas tap was left on. When accidentally ignited by a junior chef, a fireball blasted into the extraction system. The flames quickly spread and threatened to engulf the whole building and, though the fire brigade managed to contain it, the roof and ancient timber joists quickly became a charred mess. Thankfully the ground floor and conservatory only suffered water damage and, within days, the pub was back serving Fuller's beers.

The Dove is listed in *The Guinness Book of Records* for having the smallest bar in Britain with dimensions of just 1.3 x 2.4m (4.2 x 7.8ft). In addition, there is a comfortable riverside garden, a low-ceilinged lounge where tall drinkers run the risk of banging their heads and a conservatory with a vine. The pub gets very busy in summer. The food is a combination of traditional classics; pork belly is currently popular and there's a selection of contemporary dishes. In the warmer months people dine alfresco on the riverside terrace with its great views of the Thames.

Many 'greats' have drunk here, including Dylan Thomas, Graham Greene, Ernest Hemingway and Alec Guinness, and Charles II visited with Nell Gwynne. The poet James Thomson is thought to have written 'Rule Britannia' while lodging here.

The Rutland Ale House

15 Lower Mall, Hammersmith, W6 9DJ

BEERS: Fuller's London Pride, plus a changing range of cask ales

It might look old-fashioned from the outside but inside it is smart, comfortable and the place for a party

From Hammersmith Bridge, as the evening darkens, the Rutland shines on Lower Mall. It is a large, imposing pub with an old-fashioned exterior. Its large windows create an impressive atmosphere, which give way to a modern interior with wooden floors, sofas and a carpeted dining area. The Rutland is brasher and the customers often younger than those in the adjacent Blue Anchor. It is a good-time, fun place with plenty of benches outside, being ideal for watching straining rowers carrying their boats out of the rowing club next door.

Furnival Gardens are just up river. They were created in 1951 for the Festival of Britain on a former bombsite. The festival celebrated the UK's recovery after World War II, though it really highlighted London's regeneration. In earlier times, fishermen would have moored here until the beginning of the nineteenth century because the gardens are located in what was once the mouth of the navigable Hammersmith Creek.

For lovers of the Arts and Crafts Movement, Kelmscott House in Upper Mall is well worth visiting. The home of William Morris, the artist and designer who lived here until his death in 1896, it's now the headquarters of the William Morris Society with a museum in the basement and coach house. It contains a changing exhibition of Morris embroideries and Pre-Raphaelite drawings. William Morris said that the garden is the most beautiful in London. Though rarely open to the public you can glimpse it from the Upper Mall.

Blue Anchor

13 Lower Mall, Hammersmith, W6 9DJ

BEERS: Blue Anchor Ale and Sambrook's, plus at least three guest ales

If the inside of the Blue Anchor is crowded with people there is normally room at the tables on the Thames path outside

No surprise that a pub associated with the sea should be called the Blue Anchor. This riverside pub is on the route of the annual Oxford and Cambridge Boat Race from its start by Putney Bridge to the finish at Mortlake. On race day, drinkers spill out of this smallish pub onto the riverside. The inside is intimate and has the feel of a well-heeled but much-used rowing club with blades and oars hanging from the ceiling. The upstairs River Room has great views of the river and a lovely spot to have a leisurely meal. The walls are adorned with an eclectic range of historic prints and photos of the area.

The pub was licensed in 1722 and Gustav Holst (who was musical director at St Paul's Girls' School in nearby Brook Green) wrote the 'Hammersmith Suite' here. It is unlikely that the pub has changed much since then. There are marvellous views over the river, St Paul's Boys' School can be seen through the trees and to the left is Hammersmith Bridge. Over the bridge is the Wetlands Centre, an exceptional nature reserve in central London, built on 105 acres of old reservoirs. The original Hammersmith Bridge was the first suspension bridge over the Thames and was built from 1833 to 1837. It was replaced by Sir Joseph Bazalgette's design and is now the handsomest river crossing along the Thames.

Heading west, it is possible to enjoy a riverside walk that takes in the Fuller's Lion Brewery, in Chiswick, the last of London's big brewery firms. Young's, in Wandsworth, closed some years ago with production moving to Bedford, and the giant former Anheuser Busch Brewery in Mortlake now stands silent. Beers from one of London's new wave of craft brewers, Sambrook's, which is based in Wandsworth, are served in the Dove. Its Wandle Junction beer, named after a local railway junction, has a deep amber colour and spicy hop flavour with bold citrus overtones that comes from the use of Challenger, Bramling Cross and Goldings hops. The brewery uses whole hops rather than a hop oil extract to give a greater, deeper flavour.

The Crabtree Tavern

Rainville Road, Fulham, W6 9HA

BEERS: changing range of cask ales

Recently refurbished, it has a warm welcoming atmosphere, which is well loved by its many locals

The owner of The Crabtree says he wants it to be a home-from-home for those living in the capital. On the riverbank between Hammersmith and Putney bridges, the pub has a splendid beer garden with a glazed colonnade and graceful weeping willows, and offers impressive views of the Thames. Built in 1898 this large Victorian building has recently been refurbished and oozes style; it retains much of its original character and charm, carefully melding it with modern chic. Close to Craven Cottage, the home of Fulham football club, the pub is a 10-minute stroll from Hammersmith underground station along the Thames Path.

The food is firmly in the gastropub category and includes roasted quail and Devon crab cakes. The pub is renowned for its Sunday roasts, with many guests making an afternoon of their meal, reading papers and chatting. On warmer days there is a barbecue outside. The pub is one of the last places where you can play 'Devil among the tailors', a form of table skittles with a ball on a string.

The pub used to be known as the Pot House and later as The Three Jolly Gardeners. Before becoming a pub there could have been a lime works on the site with a pot kiln for making the lime, or even a maltings where grain would be prepared for the brewing industry. Nearby is Fulham Palace Road Cemetery with its impressive nineteenth-century architecture. By the gates is a large gothic crypt complete with dramatic buttresses and gargoyles, and inside the cemetary are many magnificent commemorative tombs.

Duke's Head

8 Lower Richmond Road, Putney, SW15 1JN

BEERS: Wells & Young's

A fine example of a Victorian pub which more than suits today's tastes of style and comfort

The front bar of this smart, hard-working pub has commanding views over the Thames and is at its busiest on Oxford and Cambridge Boat Race days in April. It is said that the roar from the crowd, with its grandstand view of the universities' boathouses and the start of the race, can be heard all the way upriver at the finish in Mortlake. However, race fans will get a better view of the action from the terrace of Ye White Hart (see page 72).

The original 1832 Duke's Head was rebuilt in 1864, and further altered in 1894, and has always been a Young's pub. It is the kind of pub that Young's are so good at running, large and stylish but with space to suit almost every possible taste. The pub still has much of its original ornate glass, polished woodwork and smart Victorian fireplaces. The food is adventurous pub grub and includes fillet steaks, braised pork belly and grilled fish. Younger drinkers particularly enjoy the back bar and newly refurbished basement, and it is said to be the place where many a young man takes his future wife on a first date. Because of its location it is busy virtually all year round. In summer, drinkers stand on the footpath and even further across the street until passing walkers, joggers and cyclists and customers merge to become one big throng.

Part of the pub's charm, and the reason why it can serve many people quickly, is the large, elaborate bar. Island bars were very much a mid-Victorian innovation and owe their invention to the famous engineer Isambard Kingdom Brunel. Passengers travelling on Brunel's Great Western Railway often faced a wait at Swindon, but the bar was too small to serve all the passengers before the train continued its journey. Brunel realized that an island bar was the ideal solution. The idea caught on and boosted the trend of the 1870s and 1880s for pubs to be divided into rooms and snugs.

The Bricklayer's Arms

32 Waterman Lane, Putney, SW15 1DD

BEERS: usually has 12 real ale pumps, including beers from Dark Star, Downton and West Berkshire

A real-ale paradise, it is the only pub in London to stock the full range of Timothy Taylor beers

The Bricklayer's Arms is a survivor, situated down a side street, a few moments' walk from Putney Bridge. Surrounded by larger pubs, all with finer views over the river, it is a small fish in a big pond but, when it comes to real ale, its reputation dwarfs its corporate rivals. It has won many accolades including the Campaign for Real Ale's London Pub of the Year, quite an honour as the capital has more than 5,000 pubs.

Built in 1826 on the site of an old coaching house and blacksmith's forge, it was frequented by river workers. At the end of the nineteenth century it was renamed the Bricklayer's, recognizing the changing face of London and the massive building programme being undertaken nearby. Builders met at the pub to get work and be paid. The brickies had their own bar while the bosses drank in the adjacent saloon.

Over the years the pub went through many changes and makeovers but, by 2000, its future looked bleak. London's many back-street pubs had become more valuable to developers as sites for modern flats. Two locals, Helen and John Marklew, who loved the pub's quirkiness, lack of pretentiousness and creaking beauty, managed to buy the pub at an auction saving it from developers. It ran as a pub for a while but they couldn't make it viable, and it became the family home. In 2005, after Helen's death, her sister, the actress Becky Newman, offered to run it as a pub again to help the family raise some money. She gave up her life on the boards for the bare floorboards of the Bricklayers. It opened on Boat Race day, was an instant success and people have been flocking to this fabulous pub ever since.

Inside there's a single basic bar and a long gallery, with seating to suit people of all sizes and tastes. The owner likes to feature beers from a different brewer each week and tries to find ones that are not normally sold anywhere else in London. One of its highlights is a hugely successful annual regional beer festival, which spills out from the bar into the paved back garden.

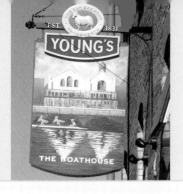

The Boathouse

Brewhouse Lane, Putney, SW15 2JX

BEERS: Wells & Young's

A busy, modern, stylish pub and bar which makes fantastic use of the space in an old Victorian building

This is a pub with verve and vigour that, on dark evenings, shimmers and sparkles from the other side of the river. It 'shines', as songwriter Paul Simon says, 'like a national guitar'.

At the merest hint of good weather the large terrace is quickly packed, hardly surprising when The Boathouse – a heady cocktail of brashness and sophistication – has some of the best views of the Thames. Situated between the railway bridge with its pedestrian walkway and the clamour of Putney Bridge, the pub company Young's has taken a utilitarian Victorian building and married it with ski lodge chic. A stunning glass front has been added that makes both looking in and out easy on the eye, just like many of the customers.

Split into three levels, there's a downstairs bar to stand and chat and an upstairs with space, comfortable sofas, armchairs, high ceilings and stylish decorations. The top floor, which is only a few moments' walk away from the bustle of Putney's main drag, must be one of the finest venues for members of the party generation who live in some of the adjoining apartments that form part of this new wharf development.

South-west London is blessed with many fine pubs, and this new development proves that real ale and young people, in fact any one enjoying the riverside, do mix in a contemporary setting. The food is modern and wholesome – chunky chips with Exmoor beef burgers, and home-made salmon fishcakes are favourites. The draught ales come from Wells & Young's in Bedford. Young's was once a London brewer, but the difficulty of running a brewery and spiralling London property prices persuaded the company to merge its brewing with Bedford favourite Charles Wells and leave the capital, leaving it free to concentrate its management skills on running pubs. On a sunny afternoon, as the crowd grows and the terrace area turns into a happy gathering, there can be few better experiences than a glass of Young's Bitter – a wonderfully refreshing beer with a hint of citrus flavours.

CHELSEA TO TOWER BRIDGE

Once Chelsea was a Saxon village miles away from the thriving bustle of the City of London, situated near where Tower Bridge now stands. Today, upbeat, upmarket Chelsea is right in the centre of things. The river passes some of London's greatest landmarks, including the Palace of Westminster, London Eye, St Paul's and the Tower, and apartment and office blocks claw their way into the sky. But even here the river is still a haven for wildlife – birds are drawn to it and, beneath its surface, fish once again can be found.

1. The Cat's Back
2. The Ship
3. The Waterfront
4. The Cross Keys
5. The Waterside
6. The Riverside
7. Morpeth Arms
8. Tamesis Dock
9. Doggett's Coat & Badge
10. The Black Friar
11. Founders Arms
12. The Pepys
13. The Banker
14. Old Thameside Inn
15. The Anchor
16. The Market Porter
17. The Mudlark
18. The Rake
19. The Barrowboy and Banker
20. The Homiman At Hay's
21. The Dickens Inn

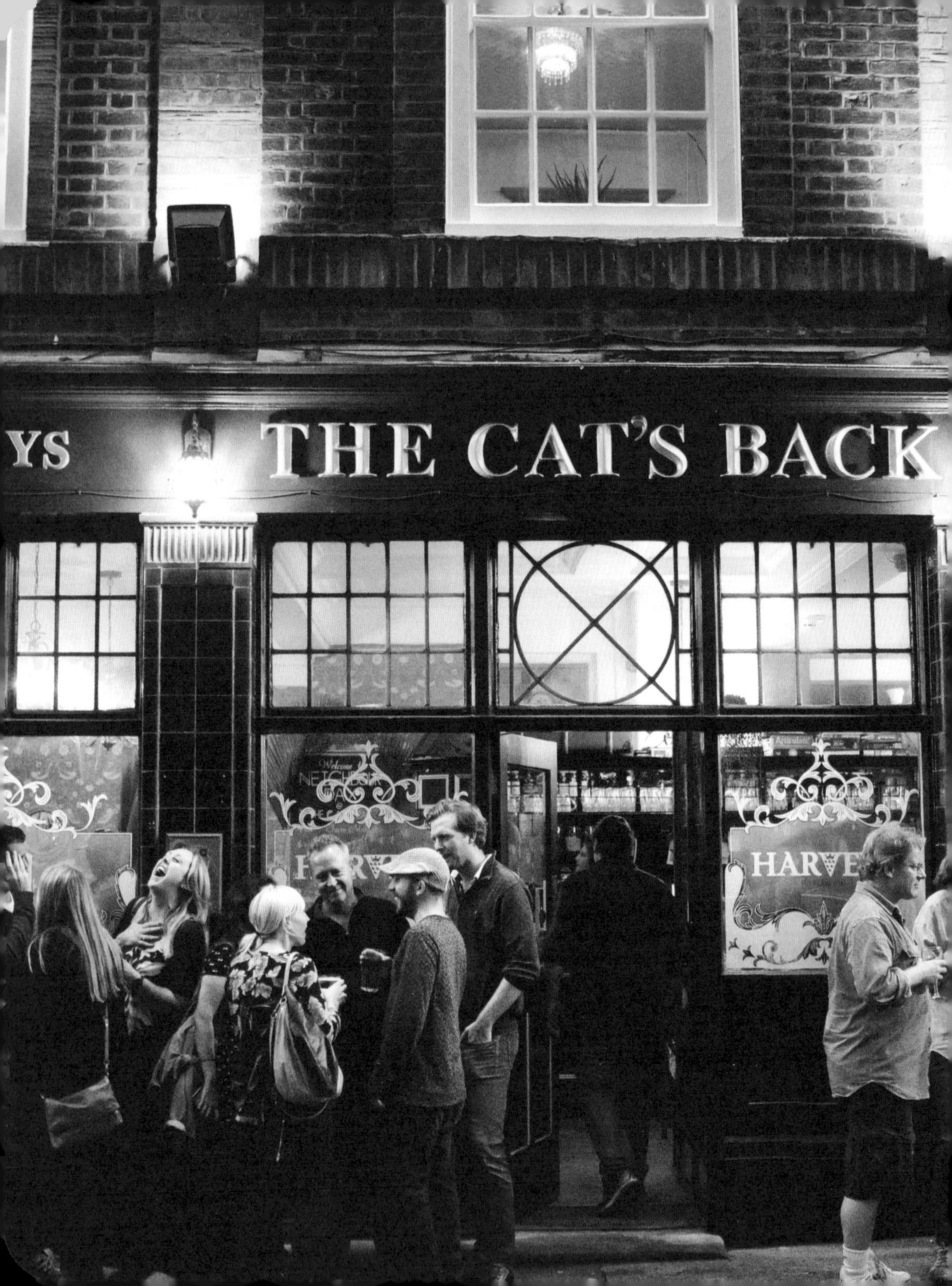
YS
THE CAT'S BACK
HARVE

The Cat's Back

86-88 Point Pleasant, Wandsworth, SW18 1NN

BEERS: Harveys

A popular local pub, which is owned by Sussex brewer Harveys. It's a little bit of the countryside in the heart of town.

Can there be a better street corner pub? There is something endearingly attractive about this pub. Even its name is eccentric. Built in 1865, it was called Ye Olde House and Home and provided a place where lightermen from the Thames and Wandle could drink pints of liquid bread. At some time the landlord's moggy went walkabout. After a month's absence, it returned – and the rest they say is history.

The pub is a survivor, standing shoulder to shoulder with row upon row of luxury apartments. It was bought by Sussex brewer Harveys in 2012. This backstreet boozer is a hidden gem amidst the high rises of Wandsworth. Recently refurbished, the bright and airy front bar is cosy and comfortable with a bohemian community atmosphere, which is in keeping with the pub's local, communal and traditional roots.

This Victorian survivor now nestles in the new riverside quarter between Wandsworth and Putney in South West London. The pub recently won a joint first place in the Campaign for Real Ale's National Pub Design Awards, receiving the Joe Goodwin Award for the Best Corner Street Local. Upstairs allows for more space and privacy away from the front bar area, with a dual use function room.

A small, decked beer garden is out the back, and it is only a five-minute walk from the ever moving Thames. It is a local pub, which welcomes visitors. Wednesday is free film night in the upstairs room, and Thursdays are given over to live music, usually acoustic traditional music from around the world.

The food is wholeheartedly pubby, rather than foodie, but that doesn't stop it being memorable. Homemade pies and tarts, hearty sandwiches, seasonal soups, daily specials, traditional desserts and Sunday roasts are the order of the day. And for anyone who likes ale, what could be better than a glass of Harveys Sussex Bitter? Full bodied and golden brown, its aroma of swirling Goldings hops is in near perfect balance with the barley malt in the beer.

The Ship

41 Jew's Row, Wandsworth, SW18 1TB

BEERS: Wells & Young's

One of West London's best known pubs The Ship is renowned for its good food, great beer and party atmosphere

People like to party at The Ship, and when the temperature creeps up or the sun comes out, the staff fire up the outside barbecue and the fun begins on the large deck overlooking the Thames. You can eat burgers, king prawns, tuna steak, surf and turf, monkfish and halibut skewers while a jazz band often plays. Inside it is comfortable and spacious, with an impressive round stove in the centre of the bar. An open kitchen prepares imaginative modern dishes for the comfortable restaurant and bar. The Ship is famed for its crispy pork belly and sticky toffee puddings. There are large mirrors and a mixture of standing and seating space for large groups, with nooks and crannies for more intimate conversations.

The Ship's exterior might look unprepossessing, but it is one of south-west London's best-known pubs with a vibrant atmosphere. It overlooks Wandsworth Bridge, is close to Wandsworth train station and shines like a beckoning lighthouse. The building dates from at least 1809 and was first leased by Young & Co in 1832, before they bought it outright in 1897 in an area then known as Bridge Field, which also had a public dock, which anyone on the river could use. Once two cottages stood between the Ship and the river, but they were bought and demolished in 1857 and have been replace by the pub's conservatory and garden.

The Waterfront

Baltimore House, Juniper Drive, Wandsworth, SW18 1TS

BEERS: Wells & Young's

A modern development offering fantastic views of Putney Bridge and Chelsea Harbour

Built beneath a stunning property development just a few metres away from Wandsworth Bridge, it is open and airy and built on several floors, with light flooding in through the large expanse of windows. The marvel of contemporary architecture is that it often asks the question, what on earth is holding up the ceiling because the glazing seems to run unimpaired from floor to roof?

The panoramic views from the upstairs balcony stretch from Putney Bridge to Chelsea Harbour, the City and beyond, and are especially dramatic at night. The pub delivers precisely what its name says, with a large terrace outside that gets very crowded on sunny days. The food is what you'd expect from a Young's pub with fancy burgers, beer-battered fish and chips, fried sea bass and pasta dishes. In addition there are pub quiz nights, poker evenings and a jazz band once a week.

Once this area was known as Gargoyle Wharf, and was the site of a Shell oil terminal and distillery; gin was made here and the pub's address makes it quite clear what was used as a flavouring. Today the area is more upmarket and known as Battersea Reach. A property development has pushed industry aside. In 1996, before the development was built, it was the site of an eco-protest known as Pure Genius that campaigned for affordable housing. The Diggers-style protest drew its inspiration from the time after the English Civil War when the defeated king no longer owned all the land. In 1649 a group of poor and landless families in Walton-on-Thames met on St George's Hill and began cultivating some common ground. They argued that no one should go hungry while others grew rich, and that the enclosure of the land underpinned an unjust class system.

The Cross Keys

1 Lawrence Street, Chelsea, SW3 5NB

BEERS: Greene King IPA and usually a guest beer from a local brewer

The Cross Keys is a stylish pub and a fine restaurant which has a most unusual façade

For too long, because of upward spiralling property prices, London has been a battleground between property developers who want to buy pubs and turn them into luxury apartments and people trying to save their local. The developers usually win. But, not so in the case of The Cross Keys.

It has been a difficult few years for the pub, as its future was fought out in the courts. It stood empty and then was taken over by squatters. Since March 2015, however, it has been a pub again. A new operator was given a long lease on the bar and dining room, and for now its future looks secure.

The oldest pub in Chelsea, founded in 1708, it has had some notable customers, including the artists Dante Gabriel Rossetti, James Whistler and William Holman Hunt. Members of the Rolling Stones, Bob Marley and author Agatha Christie have drunk here too. Much of the original interior was destroyed, but thousands of pounds have been spent to make the interior a pub again. The walls were stripped back and the space has been filled with ornamental eighteenth- and nineteenth-century antiques, including large wooden shutters from a Portuguese asylum and vintage streetlights from Paris. The decor gives the pub a contemporary look from the cosy old fireplace through to the natural light of the back atrium. Beers from many of London's new wave of brewers are showcased, and the menu is modern English from stylish Scotch eggs and sausage rolls through to oysters when in season. Other menu stars include grilled calves liver, roast lamb shoulder and a tempura lobster burger.

There is also a small shop on site, which sells homemade jams, chutneys and sauces made in the pub's kitchen.

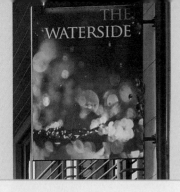

The Waterside

Riverside Tower, Imperial Wharf, Fulham, SW6 2SU

BEERS: Wells & Young's

The Waterside is a fine example of a modern, newly-built pub in one of London's smartest neighbourhoods

The Waterside is both a pub and gastropub situated in a superb location in Fulham's Imperial Wharf. It is the place to have a beer with mates, a quick brunch with a friend, an indulgent evening meal or a leisurely Sunday lunch. The food is bright and modern, international with an English twist and includes fishcakes with a mango and mint salsa, racks of lamb and battered fish and chips.

Next to Chelsea Harbour, and the river taxis up to the City, it is also close to Imperial Wharf Station. It is situated within walking distance of Kings Road, once the hippest street in London. Kings Road runs from Fulham to Sloane Square, which is the home of the Royal Court Theatre and the Peter Jones department store that was built in 1936 and was one of the first structures in Britain to have an impressive glass front.

It's now a Grade II listed building. Until 1830 Kings Road was a private road used by successive monarchs en route to Kew or Hampton Court. In the 1960s it became famous for its fashionable boutiques and the fashion designers Mary Quant and Vivienne Westwood, and was synonymous with swinging London, matched only by Carnaby Street in London's West End. It has a certain Bohemian quality because at one time many famous artists lived just south of the road, on the river at Cheyne Walk.

The pub is close to the 10-acre Imperial Park, that was built when the area was redeveloped. It is the first new public park of its size to be completed in London for 50 years, and incorporates a tree-lined avenue, extensive grassed areas, formal planting, a boating pond and children's play area.

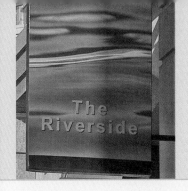

The Riverside

5 St George's Wharf, Vauxhall, SW8 2LE

BEERS: Wells & Young's

The Riverside forms part of a stylish new development that has brought life back to this part of London

The Riverside represents all that is good about the new, smart, suave and swaggeringly sophisticated London. The pub is stylish and, like the Boathouse in Putney, was built as part of as a development of luxury flats and offices. Inside are leather sofas, wooden floors, smart dining chairs and tables, and a large glass front. The ales are from the Wells & Young's range, though a guest beer is normally on sale. The food is typically modern English with a continental twist. Outside the Riverside a sign says, 'This site has been worshipped, feared, respected, worked, abused, traversed, ignored, restored and enjoyed'. And certainly many people enjoy the bar's stylish patio, with its large tables and umbrellas. A jazz band often plays on Sundays.

The pub's bar offers sweeping views of the London Eye, the steel and granite Vauxhall Bridge that opened in 1906, and the four classical column-shaped towers of the former Battersea Power Station, one of London's best-known industrial landmarks. The largest brick building in Europe, it has celebrity status having featured on the cover of Pink Floyd's 1977 album *Animals* and in the Beatle's 1965 film *Help*. The future of this iconoclastic Grade II listed building, which provided electricity to Londoners for more than 50 years, is now in doubt. Unused since 1982, it stands empty and derelict. The building was designed in the 1930s by Sir Giles Gilbert Scott, whose other work includes Liverpool Cathedral, Waterloo Bridge and the classic red telephone box.

The nearest underground station is Vauxhall, just a few moments away. It stands opposite New Covent Garden Market, which has been dubbed the 'Larder of London'. The market, which is the largest wholesale fruit and vegetable market in the UK, moved to this site from Covent Garden in 1974. From this 55-acre site comes much of London's fruit, vegetables, flowers, shellfish and ice for restaurants, hotels, etc. It opens at 3am but closes before the first pints of the day are poured at the Riverside. A general market and car boot sale for the public is held at the market on Sundays, opening at 8am.

Morpeth Arms

58 Millbank, Pimlico, SW1P 4RW

BEERS: Wells & Young's

Morpeth Arms has to have one of the most graceful exteriors of any pub in London – it is a Grade II listed building

The inside is as handsome as the grand exterior. The former is decorated in mahogany and glass while the downstairs bar has the comfortable feel of a room well used to animated conversation. Upstairs is the elegant and curvaceous Spying Room that offers impressive views over the Thames and the smart pleasure cruisers. It is decorated with photographs of the Cambridge Five, an infamous ring of spies, including Anthony Blunt and Kim Philby, who spied for Russia throughout the 1940s and early 1950s. The room's name is also a reminder that across the river stands the impressive headquarters of MI5, the UK's secret service.

When the pub was built it was next to the Penitentiary (a prison), then on the site of the current Tate Britain. The prison was based on a design (called a panopticon) by the philosopher Jeremy Bentham. It featured prisoners held in separate cells on different landings so that they could all be watched from a central point. The place had a fearful reputation, and barges took prisoners to the ocean-going ships that would transport them to Australia.

The pub is named after the chief commissioner responsible for the development of the area, Viscount Morpeth. Built by the pub designer Paul Dangerfield in 1845, on what had been marshland, it is now a Grade II listed building. The task of draining the area fell to the great engineer and master builder Thomas Cubitt, who built and funded nearly 1km (0.6 miles) of the Thames Embankment. Cubitt's other achievements did much to add to the grace and grandeur of London: in 1820 he developed Gordon Square and Tavistock Square, and in 1824 he was commissioned by Grosvenor Estates to build Belgrave Square and Pimlico. He was also responsible for the east side of Buckingham Palace.

Tamesis Dock

Albert Embankment, Vauxhall, SE1 7TP

BEERS: Greene King Abbot ale plus large and changing list of beers from regional brewers

Finding a pub in a former barge is unusual, but then the Tamesis Dock is full of surprises

Occasionally, even walking along the Thames can seem lacklustre. The stretch between Vauxhall and Lambeth bridges feels muted, so to chance upon a former, nearly 80-year-old Dutch barge, which spent most of its working life on canals on the continent, adds a bit of fun. This bar and restaurant that doubles as a music venue was once known as the English Maid and is now called the Tamesis Dock. Drinkers can sit on the deck, which is often so busy that customers need to be very patient when waiting to be served. Alternatively sit downstairs in one of the two lower decks, which also have bars. The beer range might not be inspired, but the views of the Houses of Parliament and London Eye are, especially at night when the lights spiral into the darkness or sparkle on the water.

The bar's name is derived from an ancient (possibly Celtic) name for the river, and it might have had a religious significance. About 58km (36 miles) west, in Henley-on-Thames, there's a bridge built in 1786 with statues created by sculptor Anne Seymour Damer. They show a god-like Tamesis looking upstream while Isis, the name of the Thames above Oxford, looks downstream.

Doggett's Coat & Badge

1 Blackfriars Bridge, Southwark, SE1 9UD

BEERS: a wide range of cask beers from regional and small breweries across the UK

An eighteenth-century Irish actor has given his name to this commanding riverside pub which was built in the 1970s

Doggett's Coat and Badge is the prize and name of the oldest rowing race in the world, and it's believed to be the oldest sporting contest in continued existence. It has been held every year since 1715 on the Thames between London Bridge and Cadogan Pier in Chelsea, with six young waterman racing the 6.6km (4 mile 5 furlong) course for a coat and silver badge. The race's benefactor was Thomas Doggett, an eighteenth-century theatre impresario and manager at Drury Lane and Haymarket theatres who, according to legend, created the race having been rescued from the Thames by a waterman, the equivalent of a modern taxi driver. However, the truth is probably more prosaic; betting on the outcome of boat races was then common and Doggett is known to have liked a flutter. On his death in 1721, he left money in his will to set up a trust ensuring the race continues to this day.

The pub itself rises like the soaring decks of a concrete and stone liner moored on the south bank of Blackfriars Bridge. Built in 1976, the pub has four bars on different floors, each with a different character, and includes a sports bar and a restaurant, but the best place to enjoy the sweeping views of the other side of the river is from the terrace. Given its prominence on the Thames Path, the pub is often mobbed with drinkers. Incidentally, Blackfriars Bridge was opened in 1899 by Queen Victoria. The bridge was originally named after William Pitt, the Tory prime minister. However, the name was so unpopular it was changed to Black Friars, an order of monks that settled in London in 1279. A rail bridge once ran beside the bridge and the remains of it, the red columns in the river and the insignia of the railway company, can still be seen.

The Black Friar

174 Queen Victoria St, Blackfriars, EC4V 4EG

BEERS: cask beers from some of the UK's smallest regional and local brewers

The curious interior and exterior of The Black Friar was inspired by the work of artist and socialist William Morris

The exterior of this narrow, wedge-shaped pub is intriguing if seemingly uninspired, especially at street level. But a glance at the statue of a jolly monk above the door only hints at the drama that lies inside. From 1880 to 1910 a generation of writers, designers and architects were influenced by the Arts and Crafts Movement, instigated by the artist and socialist William Morris. Using a medieval style of decoration, it advocated craftsmanship and truth to materials. The style has much in common with the contemporary art nouveau, and it played a role in the founding of Bauhaus and modernism. The narrow end of the somewhat dark pub assumes the air of a pseudo-baronial hall, which leads to a sumptuous, intimate room at the back.

Many thought that the Arts and Craft Movement was somewhat prosaic but The Black Friar is the cure. Friezes in copper, marble and plaster show monks enjoying themselves. One is about to boil an egg, some are singing and others collect fish and eels to eat on meatless days. Above are signs containing aphorisms such as 'finery is foolery', 'don't advertise, or tell a gossip', 'haste is slow', and a 'good thing is soon snatched up'. There are more than 50 different types of marble in the building that, with its stylized light fittings, furniture and wood carvings, means it is far more than a just a pub. The interior is unique and deserves to be preserved. It is hard to believe that in the 1960s the pub faced being demolished and replaced by an office block.

The pub's décor is an elaborate fanciful joke. A sign above the bar suggests that this is where the Holy Roman Emperor Charles V, the Papal Legate and Henry VIII met to discuss Henry's divorce from Catherine of Aragon. Or perhaps they did. The site of the pub was a Dominican friary from 1279 to the Reformation in 1539, but such a meeting would have surely have made the monks scowl.

Founders Arms

52 Hopton Street, Southwark, SE1 9JH

BEERS: Wells & Young's

A modern pub on the south bank of the river, it offers impressive views of St Paul's and is next to the Tate Modern

There cannot be many pubs that offer customers a blanket, but for those who want to sit outside on the coldest days the Founders is your place. Situated on the river next to Tate Modern at the south side of the Millennium Bridge, this contemporary, glass-fronted pub has a large patio overlooking St Paul's Cathedral.

The Tate Modern is one of four Tate Galleries; there's Tate Britain in London, Tate Liverpool and Tate St Ives in Cornwall. Tate Modern is housed in the former Bankside power station that was built in two phases between 1947 and 1963. It was designed by Sir Giles Gilbert Scott who was also the architect of Battersea Power Station, Liverpool Cathedral and the designer of the famous British red telephone box. Standing opposite St Paul's, the power station was conceived as a new kind of cathedral, a cathedral of pure energy. Inside, where

once giant turbines whirled and produced electricity for London, is now the national collection of international modern art created since 1900. The Globe Theatre is nearby.

Once medieval palaces stood on the banks of this stretch of the Thames. The rich chose it as the place to display their opulence. Bankside also became the residence for the Bishop of Winchester. But by the end of the nineteenth century it was a place of industry and commerce and the home of thousands of people, many of whom lived in abject poverty. There was a gas works, an iron foundry, glass making, a coconut fibre works, a boiler works, a vinegar distillery, breweries and wharves lining the river. All of this is hard to imagine – even if wrapped in a blanket, sitting by a patio heater while enjoying the sumptuous views and a pint of Bombardier Bitter.

The Pepys

Stew Lane, Mansion House, EC4V 3PT

BEERS: a wide range of cask beers

A sociable pub, which during the week is busy with City workers out for a quick lunch or relaxing at the end of their working day

The entrance down a narrow lane off Upper Thames Street might seem a little unprepossessing, but inside The Pepys is quite a find. It is an impressive stylish bar and restaurant, a five-minute walk from Sir Christopher Wren's masterpiece, St Paul's Cathedral. Comfortable and modern inside with lots of polished wood and unpainted brickwork, it offers a relaxing way to way to watch the Thames while having a drink and something to eat. There is a balcony that overhangs the river. The sweeping views are a big draw and take in the Shard, Globe Theatre, Tate Modern and the Millennium Bridge.

Set in an old warehouse, it fronts the Thames and gives magnificent views. The bar still retains many features of the original warehouse, though it has been knocked into one floor. Pillars, warehouse windows and London stock brick walls are all found in this stylish bar. The menu includes many variations on steaks and burgers, but there are also some pretty good stone-baked pizzas and lots of boards for sharing for those who want something lighter. In the evening, it is not uncommon to find it full of city workers sipping on glasses of sparkling wine or cocktails. Surprisingly for a pub with this name, there is little inside to link it to the seventeenth-century diarist Samuel Pepys. But Pepys, with his love of life, would probably have adored this place.

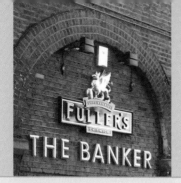

The Banker

Cousin Lane, Cannon Street, EC4R 3TE

BEERS: Fuller's

The Banker is very much a city pub and often closes early in the evening when the office workers go home

Not far from Southwark Bridge, down a side street beside Cannon Street Station, the Banker is not always easily found. The pub is under one of the sweeping brick arches under the station and, at times, the froth on top of a pint of Fuller's London Pride actually seems to vibrate as a commuter train rumbles overhead, taking workers back to south and east London.

Inside the pub there are smaller archways with sofas for lounging on. It is the type of pub that offers space for large groups and nooks and crannies for those wanting something more intimate. The expansive brickwork décor is punctuated by dramatic black-and-white photographs of river life. The veranda offers sweeping views from London Bridge to Southwark Bridge and the powerful river seems tantalisingly close. Typical of many City pubs, it caters for office workers looking for a wholesome lunch in double quick time and/or a beer with friends before heading home. It is closed at the weekends.

Once this area swaggered with rich merchants who traded wines and nearby, off Upper Thames Street and near Queen Street, is Vintners Hall. In the thirteenth-century merchants would unload 'lighters' (barges) that were laden with Bordeaux wine. The original site of the Vintners Hall was bequeathed to the new livery company in 1357 and a grand hall was built. Wine was an important part the economy and culture of the period. In Norman times there was even a vineyard in the grounds of the precincts of the nearby Tower of London. The original Vintners Hall was destroyed within 24 hours of the Great Fire of London breaking out in 1666, some 600m (1,970ft) away in Pudding Lane. Rebuilt in 1671 by the master builder Roger Jarman, the Vintners was one of the 12 great City of London livery companies that, with the Dyers and the Crown, owns all the swans on the Thames. The building's impressive Thames frontage is best seen from the other side of the river.

Old Thameside Inn

Pickfords Wharf, Clink St, London Bridge, SE1 9DG

BEERS: wide range of cask ales

Once this was a warehouse for fine spices but today it's a modern, bustling pub with a great riverside terrace

There cannot be many pubs with a replica of the *Golden Hinde* outside. This ship docked here in 1996 in St Mary Overie Dock and is a full-sized reconstruction of the Tudor warship in which Sir Francis Drake circumnavigated the world in 1577-80. Built in 1973, it too has travelled the world, sailing more than 225,000km (140,000 miles). On its maiden voyage it sailed to San Francisco, replicating Drake's famous journey. However, the modern day *Hinde* did not return to England laden with treasure taken by force from Spanish vessels. Today the *Hinde* is a museum and is frequently used for films.

Nearby is the Clink Museum. The Clink was an infamous prison and its exhibits include many instruments of torture including the executioner's block, a widow's scold and the boot, a device used for crushing feet. The prison's name, which is said to come from the noise made by the many manacles and fetters used, led to the phrase 'to be in the clink', i.e. locked up in prison.

As for the pub, it's smartly decorated and split into two levels; on sunny days drinkers spill out on to the riverside veranda. A wide range of cask beers are normally available, with many customers frequently coming to taste the UK's new wave of innovative micro brewers. Today there are more than 1,500 micro-brewers in the country – and many of them are using innovative ingredients. Nicholsons – the company that owns the pub – now has a regular policy of selling beer by different producers in its pubs, with the list frequently changing.

The Anchor

34 Park Street, Bankside, SE1 9EF

BEERS: range of cask ales

A popular pub with tourists, it has close links with Samuel Pepys and Dr Johnson

There has been a pub on the site since the fifteenth century, and the current pub has been here since 1876 when it replaced a pub of the same name that burnt down. In 1666 Samuel Pepys witnessed the Great Fire of London from here. Records show that one previous name includes the Deadman's Place because there was a plague pit nearby where the bodies of the dead were buried. The pub was owned by Thrale's Brewery, which became one of the most celebrated London breweries. It dates from 1616 and, by 1750, it rivalled Truman's as the greatest porter brewhouse in London. One of the bars is named after Doctor Johnson who, in 1775, published his famous dictionary. A friend of the Thrale family, he had a room at the brewery where he wrote Lives of the English Poets.

Today's Anchor would be the perfect pub for the gregarious Johnson as it is often packed with people, enjoying the many nooks and crannies or sitting outside admiring the views of St Paul's and Tower Bridge. Popular with tourists, there is a fish-and-chip shop within the building, and the oldest and most impressive part of the building, with its low beams, exposed brickwork and open fireplaces, has been converted into tea rooms. Nearby, along the waterfront, is a recreation of Shakespeare's Globe Theatre and Tate Modern is also very close.

The Market Porter

9 Stoney Street, Southwark, SE1 9AA

BEERS: Harvey's Sussex Bitter, plus 11 guests

The pub is the perfect place to enjoy a pint of Harvey's Sussex Best Bitter while watching the world of Borough Market go by

One of London's great real-ale pubs, it is always very busy. Be prepared to stand because the seating areas inside are minimal and often there's a throng of customers outside, drinking a beer and watching the many film crews regularly at work in the area.

A pub has stood on this site since 1638, when it would have been one of the many alehouses and inns that clamoured for business along Borough High Street in the days when London Bridge was the only crossing point on the Thames to the City of London. The pub stands opposite London's finest food market, the crowded Borough Market within sight of Southwark Cathedral. A foodie's paradise, it sells just about every possible ingredient from organic Cumbrian lamb to spicy sausages from Spain and hand-made breads. A favourite brunch is freshly cooked Lincolnshire sausage, served on a slice of locally baked sourdough bread or a couple of Whitstable Bay oysters (when in season). Beer lovers should check out the Utobeer stall or visit its bar, the Rake, in Winchester Walk that sells craft beer from around the world. Or head for the Market Porter and a pint of Harvey's sublime Sussex Best Bitter, a complex beer full of citrus hop character and biscuit malt. The market has a long rich history, dating back to 1014, and probably earlier, when London Bridge attracted traders selling grain, fish, vegetables and livestock. In the thirteenth century traders were relocated to what is now Borough High Street, and a market has existed here ever since.

The Mudlark

4 Montague Close, Southwark, SE1 9DA

BEERS: wide range of cask ales

The Mudlark is a favourite in this historic part of London - it offers a fine range of ales from smaller brewers

The Mudlark is quite a find. Once it was the haunt of market porters from Borough Market but today its customers are office workers and tourists. Outside there is a fine paved beer garden, from where it is possible to enjoy the world scurrying by. The beer range is large and varied, reflecting the growing success that micro-brewers are experiencing. Sometimes the choice can seem bewildering, but the staff are well-clued up and provide samples before you buy.

The pub's name comes from an era when ragged waifs and strays scavenged the muddy Thames for coal, bits of old iron and any other loot that might have fallen off a passing ship or been thrown into the river. Today it is not unusual to see modern-day mudlarks searching the river foreshore when the tide is out. However, unlike their eighteenth-century counterparts they are dressed in protective overalls, gloves and rubber boots and use a metal detector. The findings provide us with a window into the world of medieval London. Items found range from household objects, including stools, jugs and cauldrons to cannons, frying pans, toys made of pewter, Tudor bricks, eighteenth-century clay pipes, coins, chain mail and Georgian jewellery. The thick Thames mud is low in oxygen and helps preserve the items from decay. The treasure seekers are all Society of Thames Mudlarks, a select group of specialists who have been officially approved by the Museum of London and granted licenses by the Port of London Authority. Mudlarks have to declare their finds to the Museum of London, in Docklands, which now holds over 200 such objects in its Medieval Gallery.

The Rake

14 Winchester Walk, Borough Market, Southwark, SE1 9AG

BEERS: varied but always two on draught

The Rake is for people who want to know more about great beers from the four corners of the world

When it comes to pubs, the Rake is the new brash kid on the block. It opened in 2006 on the site of a nineteenth-century public house, making it the first bar in the bounds of the Borough Market for 100 years. It was founded by Richard Dinwoodie and Michael Hill, the team behind the Utobeer stall selling beer in the market. Within a few short years the Rake has established itself as one of the best beer bars in the world and picked up several awards. The beer menu is extensive, varied and constantly changing. It always includes two draught beers and highlights have included Thomas Hardy Ale on cask (available for the first time in the UK), as well as Sierra Nevada Pale Ale from California, Veltins (a German pilsner), Maissels Weisse (a German wheat beer), plus Belgium Kwak and Liefmans Kriek.

The Rake offers more than 100 bottled beers and specials that change seasonally and include British bottle-conditioned Lambic, Trappist and champagne beers, as well as speciality beers from around the world. There's also a range of about 10 ciders including the award-winning traditional Perry's of Somerset and a wide range of schnapps, jenevers, spirits and liqueurs. New customers can be put off by the wide range, but the staff are usually very helpful and happy to discuss what's available. You don't just walk into the Rake and ask for a beer; take advice. The food is simple and includes favourites from the market such as Elizabeth King's famous pork pies, Flour Power Bread and a choice of cheeses.

The Barrowboy and Banker

6/8 Borough High Street, Southwark, SE1 9QQ

BEERS: Fuller's range

The changing face of London means that many former bank buildings have now become fine pubs

More than 750,000 people use the nearby London Bridge station each week, and at times it seems like they are all inside the pub enjoying a pint of Fuller's London Pride. It stands close to the 600-year-old Southwark Cathedral (the oldest cathedral building in London), the delights of Borough Market and the London Dungeon.

The Barrowboy and Banker was once a NatWest bank, then a wine bar and inside it still has the grandiose swagger of a temple of commerce. The ceilings are high, the pillars ornate, the windows large and an impressive staircase sweeps up to the mezzanine level. There is also a small outdoor seating area. The bar is almost sensuously curved and includes several imposing images, including the *Charge of the Scots Greys* by Lady Butler, probably the best-known painting of the attack by the Royal North Dragoons at the Battle of Waterloo in 1815. The pub is a great place for people to meet after a day's work and, for those who want something substantial to eat, it offers impressive steak-and-ale pies complete with a crunchy pastry topping.

A bridge has stood on the current site from the time of the Romans 2,000 years ago. Significantly, it is the oldest crossing point of the tidal Thames at what was the only entrance to the City of London across the river for many centuries. In medieval times shops and houses were found on the bridge, and there were so many narrow arches and wide piers slowing the flow that, in icy periods, the Thames actually froze over. Londoners took to the ice, skating, playing, riding horses and even building temporary shops. The winter of 1740 is known as 'the great frost' and the river was frozen for several weeks. Indeed, the weather was so severe that it made the movement of food and goods on the river virtually impossible, causing hardship for many poorer families.

Work began on the current bridge in 1967, replacing the iconic Rennie's bridge that was built in 1831. However, it was not the end of the old bridge – it was sold to American oil magnate Robert McCulloch who had it dismantled, brick by brick, transported across the Atlantic and rebuilt in the desert in Arizona, where it spans the entrance to a theme park and is now the state's second biggest tourist attract after the Grand Canyon.

The Horniman At Hay's

Hay's Galleria, Counter St, Southwark, SE1 2HD

BEERS: various

Part of a stunning development, which engagingly uses an eighteenth-century warehouse to create a modern shopping mall and pub

The pub is located on the riverfront and is a tribute to Frederick Horniman, a famous tea dealer. Inside murals depict his travels to Africa, India and the Americas, and clocks from his office tell the time in different parts of the world. Hay's Wharf used to be the oldest and largest in the Pool of London and was known as the 'larder of London' because so much food was landed here. Today, the river walk in front of the Horniman is packed with shoppers, tourists and office workers enjoying the dramatic views of Tower Bridge and *HMS Belfast*, which is now a museum.

Hay's Wharf, which still forms the edifice for the Galleria's elegant, covered shopping complex, was built in the 1840s by Sir William Cubitt, who also built the Bank of England. The immense brick-built, multi-level warehouses were regarded as 'the finest and best edifices of their kind in the kingdom'. In 1861 a fire ripped along the riverside from London Bridge to Hay's Wharf, lasting for almost a month and with a greater loss of life than the Great Fire of London in 1666; spectators flocked to London Bridge to watch. The wharf was rebuilt and, despite bomb damage during the Blitz, it prospered until the 1960s when the demand grew for deeper moorings for the new wave of giant container ships. The wharf fell into disrepair until the late 1980s when the area was transformed and modernized. A spectacular vaulted roof was put over the dock where once the clippers were moored. A focal point in the heart of the Galleria is David Kemp's magnificent 18m (60ft) high kinetic sculpture, *The Navigators*, which provides a soothing combination of moving parts, water jets and fountains.

The Dickens Inn

St Katharine's Dock, Tower Bridge, E1W 1UH

BEERS: Tribute, Green King IPA, Adnams

The Dickens Inn overlooks Tower Bridge and offers some stunning views of boats and the harbour

The inn opened in 1976. It is an unusual three-story wooden construction and was once a spice warehouse. It is a fun place to visit, loud and even brash but do not be put off. Each floor offers something different in the way of food, becoming more expensive as you climb the stairs.

On a bright, sunny day, it is almost impossible to believe that St Katharine's Dock, with its flotilla of luxury yachts and motorboats, is so close to the bustle of the City. It has the luxurious air and confident manner of a stopping-off point for those heading to the Mediterranean. In fact a dock has probably been on this site for 1,000 years, and the name St Katharine's was first used in Elizabethan times, but it was the industrial revolution that propelled the docks to worldwide fame. When the St Katharine Docks Bill was passed in 1825, more than £1 million was spent on creating the docks;

and the slum houses, streets and alleys with names such as Dark Entry, Cat's Hole and Pillory Lane were cleared to make way for the ambitious centre for London's industry and commerce.

Thomas Telford designed and built London's new port for commerce, and he worked with the architect Philip Hardwick on six-storey warehouses with cast-iron window frames and extensive vaults to store thousands of casks of valuable wine and other luxury goods that began to pour into the docks on a daily basis. Bomb damage in the last war and the increasing size of cargo vessels meant St Katharine's fell into disuse. But the economic renaissance in the 1970s saw the area transformed, and today it contains luxury shops, historic barges, apartments and restaurants, and is the perfect place to begin or end a riverside walk. Watching the boats use the lock is a firm favourite with many visitors.

TOWER BRIDGE SOUTHSIDE

Below the bridge the river begins the final leg of its journey to the North Sea. The Thames starts to grow wider and the gentle, flowing water becomes a river rushing towards the sea, though when the tide turns, the sea seems to rush swiftly into the capital. Once the first section of this stretch was lined with wharves and boats returning from the four corners of the world. Now long gone, the area is being regenerated with new housing developments. The river flows on past the majesty of Greenwich, a World Heritage site, and, as it heads towards the Thames Barrier, the banks become much more industrial.

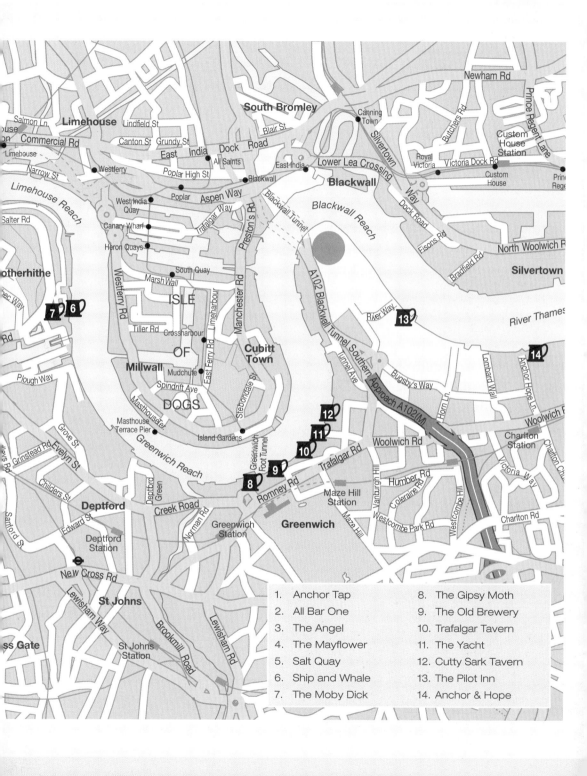

1. Anchor Tap
2. All Bar One
3. The Angel
4. The Mayflower
5. Salt Quay
6. Ship and Whale
7. The Moby Dick
8. The Gipsy Moth
9. The Old Brewery
10. Trafalgar Tavern
11. The Yacht
12. Cutty Sark Tavern
13. The Pilot Inn
14. Anchor & Hope

Anchor Tap

20 Horselydown Lane, Southwark, SE1 2LN

BEERS: Samuel Smith

For many this is the classic English pub – shunning modernization it is uncluttered, has simple food and you can play a game of darts

There is something delightfully ordinary about the Anchor Tap, which is located on the south side of the Thames close to Tower Bridge, *HMS Belfast* and the Design Museum. The pub is owned by the fiercely independent Samuel Smith Brewery from Tadcaster in North Yorkshire. Its interior is uncluttered, smart and slightly old-fashioned. The food is simple, you can play darts and drink good beer.

The pub's name gives away the fact that brewing once took place nearby. A tap is the name a brewer will use for the pub nearest the brewery, where staff can go and sample the beer. Brewing happened from the days of Queen Elizabeth until the Anchor brewery was closed in the early 1980s, though the building can still be seen squeezed between Tower Bridge and Butler's Wharf. And nearby in Borough High Street there's the former Hop Exchange where brewers and hop merchants negotiated the price for each year's harvest brought from Kent. Traditionally the first beers brewed in England were ales, and they contained no hops.

Hops act as a preservative, but their introduction to England in the fifteenth century was greeted with howls of outrage. In 1471 the brewers of Norwich were forbidden to use hops, and in 1519 another law banned the use of the 'wicked and pernicious weed, hops'. Many believed that hops could kill those who suffered from colic. However, the Reformation had a dramatic effect on brewing. About 1524 a large number of Flemish immigrants settled in Kent and started growing hops. People soon realized that beers to which hops had been added had a longer life than those without them. By the middle of the century hop growing had reached a commercial scale, leading the City of London to appoint 'hop searchers', whose job was to ensure only the best hops were used by brewers. They had the authority to destroy any hops that were not up to scratch.

All Bar One

34 Shad Thames, Butler's Wharf, SE1 2YG

BEERS: various

A thoroughly modern bar where people can engage in the age-old pastime of having a good time

The bar, with its long riverside terrace, has some of the best views of Tower Bridge and the City's financial district the other side of the river. Situated downriver from the bridge, the attractive riverside walk with its displays of anchors seems a little less frenetic than the area around London Bridge. It is appropriate that the Design Museum, which is devoted to contemporary design in every form from furniture to graphics, and architecture to industrial design, is nearby because All Bar One made its name on the strength of its design.

The bar is part of a chain, all with the same name. The concept was devised by two women who wanted to create a female-friendly pub, where women could go, perhaps on their own, without feeling uncomfortable. The design is always the same with large glass frontages, and light and airy interiors. The first of these concept bars opened in 1994 in Sutton, Surrey, and its use of natural colours, large mirrors, sofas and table service proved an instant hit; there are now about 40 of these bars in the country, all similarly decorated and with the same international menu, including tapas, baked goats cheese, burgers and salads, and usually at least one cask beer and interesting continental lagers. Highlights on the beer menu include Kasteel Cru, a zesty French beer that's fermented with champagne yeast, the strong Duvel Green Draught from Belgium and Erdinger, a refreshing German wheat beer.

The Angel

101 Bermondsey Wall East, Rotherhithe, SE16 4NB

BEERS: Samuel Smith – keg only.

Once a fallen angel nearly fell into the river. This pub is once again soaring to new heights

There is a smart and comforting austerity to the dark interior of this pub. It stands in a prime position on the embankment in Rotherhithe, with breathtaking views along the Thames towards the City and its towering office blocks. The outside looks neat and tidy but it wasn't always like this. It recently looked like it would slip shoddily into the Thames. Then it was bought by the brewer Samuel Smith who revived it. Bucking the modern trend for large, one-roomed bars, the downstairs bar was split into several areas. An upstairs room has been transformed into a smart dining lounge with a splendid view and, outside, a once tatty deck has become a comfortable place to relax. It is a pub in waiting – waiting for the surrounding area to have new life breathed into it as regeneration gets underway.

In the fifteenth century an inn stood here, built by the monks of Bermondsey Priory. There has always been a close link between the church and pubs. In medieval England monasteries would often brew beer and offer refuge to passing travellers. In the seventeenth century Samuel Pepys is said to have taken country strolls here from his home in the City. The passing of another 100 years bought wharves and docks, but then the area became a terrible slum. In the twentieth century wartime bombing and the end of London as a major seaport left this area in decline, and parts of it a wasteland. At least the Angel is back.

The Mayflower

117 Rotherhithe Street, Bermondsey, SE16 4NF

BEERS: Greene King and changing range of four guest ales

The downstairs of the pub is the perfect place to quench a thirst; hungry people eat upstairs in the restaurant

When the lights are out and the pub is dark, it is said that the voices of long-gone customers can be heard. Perhaps one belongs to Captain Christopher Jones, a journeyman sea captain and part owner of the *Mayflower*. On a summer's day in 1620, when the tide and wind were favourable, he cast off from a small nearby jetty and set sail towards the English Channel on a journey that would change the world. His passengers were religious refugees, who first had fled to Holland, but these English Puritans (who became known as the Pilgrim Fathers) were determined to seek a new life in the New World. When Jones set sail, the pub might have been called the Spread Eagle & Crown or the Shippe, but its name was changed in 1957 to The Mayflower, a move that probably saved the pub with its smart but austere interior from the ravages of property developers. The *Mayflower* and its crew returned to Rotherhithe in 1621. Jones died a year later and was buried in the nearby churchyard of St Mary's, a church designed by John James, a pupil of Sir Christopher Wren. And the fragile, much-travelled *Mayflower* was left to perish on its moorings.

The pub itself dates from the sixteenth century, though the current structure is about 200 years younger. Much of it was bomb-damaged in World War II and, though converted in the 1960s, it still has a seventeenth-century feel. There is a display of nautical items and settles with proverbs painted on. Outside there is a small deck, with limited views of the passing Thames. One of the best ways to get to the pub is to walk along the Thames path from Tower Bridge. Close by is the Brunel Museum and the Thames Tunnel, the oldest section of the London Underground, originally intended for horse-drawn carriages. When it was built (1825–1843), it was the first underwater tunnel in the world and was Isambard Kingdom Brunel's first major project.

Salt Quay

163 Old Salt Quay, Rotherhithe, SE16 5QU

BEERS: Greene King

The Salt Quay is very much a community pub, which gets busy on Sundays when families enjoy the carvery

As the Thames sweeps and swoops down river from Tower Bridge, it passes one of London's great secrets. Once Rotherhithe seemed more water than land and was the site of many docks, but now it is part of the redevelopment of the Docklands with thousands of new apartments and houses. Salt Quay is a big barn of a newish pub that was once known as Spice Island. It stands on the corner of the lock where the Thames meets Surrey Water, one of the new marinas. The views from the large terrace or from one of the galleried upper floors are fantastic. Local families like to come to the pub, many attracted by the wide and varied menu, with a carvery on Sundays. On sunny days the smell of the barbecue drifts across the terrace. Inside there are plenty of sofas with space for groups to sit. The pub is a short walk from Canada Wharf and Rotherhithe stations.

The area was extensively bombed in World War II, and the docks were drained and used to build the concrete caissons for the Mulberry Harbours (named after Mulberry Quay in the docks) used in the D-Day landings. Today the South Dock is the largest marina in London with many pleasure-sailing boats. The area also has many public sculptures: at Cumberland Wharf, near the Mayflower pub, the Bermondsey Lad and the Sunbeam Weekly, there's a series of three bronze figures – a Pilgrim Father, small boy and bull terrier, a homage to the Pilgrim Fathers. Deal Porters, a statue at Canada Water, recalls the dockers, with their special hats, who unloaded timber. In the centre of the peninsula on Stave Hill a bas-relief shows the Surrey Commercial Docks as they were in 1896. And, at Barnards Wharf, a carnival of animals parade along the riverside towards Surrey Docks Urban Farm.

Ship and Whale

2 Gulliver Street, Rotherhithe, SE16 7LT

BEERS: usually Shepherd Neame Spitfire and one guest beer

A great place to visit for anyone travelling on the Thames path

For anyone travelling along the Thames path from Greenwich to London Bridge, the Ship and Whale is an ideal stopping off place. It is also a short ferry ride from the bustle of the City or Canary Wharf. The current building was probably built in the 1880s, but a pub has been on this site since the eighteenth century. Recently restored, the pub is a hidden gem well worth finding. The Odessa Wharf building, which can be seen from the pub's sun trap garden, dates back to 1810, making it one of the oldest surviving buildings in the area. It is still a locals' pub, though today dockers are in short supply. It regularly hosts popular live-music events, barbecues and quiz nights, and serves up good wholesome pub food.

The pub is owned by Britain's oldest brewer, Shepherd Neame, which can trace its history back to 1698, though brewing began on its Faversham site many years before that. Its Spitfire bitter frequently features on the bar. Named after a famed British World War II fighter plane, the beer was first brewed in 1990 as a bottled conditioned beer to commemorate the 50th anniversary of the Battle of Britain, which took place during the summer and autumn of 1940 and saw the German Air Force pitched against the United Kingdom. Spitfire is now the brewery's flagship ale. The ale is infused with three different varieties of Kentish hops, giving it swathes of orange and pepper aromatics that cleverly balance the rich biscuit malt in the beer.

The Moby Dick

6 Russell Court East, Rotherhithe, SE16 7PL

BEERS: Fuller's

A large glass conservatory offers some fine views over the dock, it is well used by local families

This relatively new pub overlooks Greenland Dock, from where boats once sailed to Greenland, hunting whales for blubber and whalebone. It is split over two floors, with a pleasant sitting area outside, and sells the full range of Fuller's beers. The pub is named after Herman Melville's 1851 novel about Ishmael and his voyage on the whaler *Pequod*, captained by Captain Ahab, in pursuit of a giant white sperm whale. Ahab wanted revenge because the whale had caused his leg to be amputated.

Today it is hard to imagine both the importance and scale of whaling. Whale blubber was rendered down to produce oil for lamps, lubricate machinery and make soap. The bones were used in umbrellas and corsets. The sperm whale was particularly sought after as its head contained a waxy substance, spermaceti, that burns with a bright flame and was used to make the finest candles. The Moby is a friendly pub, with well-kept Fuller's beers and wholesome food, which is well used by locals. It offers some great views over the now tranquil dock, which is frequently utilized by a sailing club as well as a fisherman who sits by the water's edge, contemplating the ones that got away.

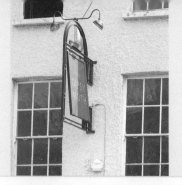

The Gipsy Moth

60 Greenwich Church Street, Greenwich, SE10 9BL

BEERS: good range of beers from London brewers

A popular tourist pub, which is close to some of Greenwich's most historic attractions

Greenwich has it all, the Royal Observatory, the *Cutty Sark*, Greenwich Park, the Nautical Museum and even World Heritage status. Once it was also home to *Gipsy Moth IV*, the boat that Sir Francis Chichester, when recuperating from illness, took on an epic journey around the world. In 1967 the 64-year-old Chichester left Plymouth to sail by himself in his 16m (52ft) long ketch. After he returned to Plymouth to national acclaim he was knighted by Queen Elizabeth II with same sword used by Queen Elizabeth I to ennoble Sir Francis Drake. On Chichester's death in 1972 *Gipsy Moth* was put on permanent display in dry dock next to the *Cutty Sark*. It became such a permanent attraction that the thousands of visitors who walked over it nearly destroyed it. It remained on display (now with 'no entry' signs) until 2003 when it was bundled onto the back of a lorry, crippled but not broken, to be restored on the Isle of Wight.

A busy tourist pub with an excellent beer garden, the Gipsy Moth is adjacent to the world's greatest clipper ship, the *Cutty Sark*, which has recently been refurbished following its gutting by fire. It's also by the entrance to the Thames Tunnel that leads walkers to and from the Isle of Dogs. More than 100 years old, the tunnel's original purpose was to allow the locals to get jobs in the docks on the north side of the river. The tunnel's entrance is marked by a glazed tower, which houses a lift down 15m (50ft) to the start of the 370m (1,215ft) long cast-iron tunnel, which is glazed with 200,000 white tiles.

The Old Brewery

The Pepys Building, The Old Royal Naval College, Greenwich, SE10 9LW

BEERS: Meantime

A thoroughly modern pub and restaurant which has bought brewing back to the historic site of the Old Royal Naval College

The Royal Hospital's Old Brewery has been brought back to use after 140 years by Meantime Brewing Company. The Old Brewery is in the grounds of the Old Royal Naval College, part of the spectacular World Heritage Site of Maritime Greenwich, and is a stone's throw from the world's last tea clipper, the legendary *Cutty Sark*. The brewery once supplied the pensioners of the Royal Naval Hospital with a two-quart daily ration of beer and is now a restaurant, bar and café with a micro-brewery creating historical and modern beers. The Old Brewery was built on the foundations of a brewhouse built by Joseph Kay in 1832; it was rebuilt after a fire in 1843 but, by 1870, was no longer in use.

Today, eight 1,000 litre (220 gallon) copper-clad tanks dominate the main hall of The Old Brewery, clearly visible to the diners. The spirit of the brewhouse is kept alive through the use of ancient recipes and ingredients, such as bog myrtle and wormwood, while there are also avant-garde beers, including Mojito Pilsners and Juniper Pale Ales, specifically crafted to match the flavours and aromas of the modern cuisine.

Meantime's founder Alastair Hook created a signature beer for the venue, a deeply flavoured, restorative Hospital Porter. Brewed to a 1750s recipe and matured for a minimum of one year, it is an oak-aged London Porter with an 8 per cent ABV and is packed with rich malt, liquorice, chocolate and caramel flavours. Adjoining the main hall is a cosy annexe bar and tranquil courtyard. Displayed against the exposed brickwork are the beer bottle

and glass collections of the seminal beer writer, the late Michael Jackson, known as the Beer Hunter, an early fan and great supporter of Meantime. The brewery is located within the Discover Greenwich complex, which uses state of the art techniques to tell the story of Maritime Greenwich and the Old Royal Naval College. Over 500 years of history from Henry VIII's Tudor Palace, Wren's Royal Hospital for Seamen and the Royal Naval College is explored.

Trafalgar Tavern

Park Row, Greenwich, SE10 9NW

BEERS: Adnams, Sharps

If only more pubs were like the Trafalgar – it offers great food, good beer, fabulous views and a real sense of history

Charles Dickens is to London what James Joyce is to Dublin, except Dickens' London is one of dark shadows, labyrinths and intrigues. Today, the insanitary slums are long gone but you can still sit where his sometime heroic and often unsavoury characters supped ale. One of the most potent symbols in Dickens' *Our Mutual Friend* is that of the River Thames – its flowing waters are a sign of renewal and rebirth, and it is here at the Trafalgar that the book's central characters, Bella Wilfer and John Rokesmith, held their wedding feast.

The Trafalgar stands like a piece of crumbling, iced cake, faded but not down. It is famed for its whitebait dinners often held upstairs in the Lord Nelson Room with its sweeping view of the curve in the Thames, the Isle of Dogs and towards the O2. In the nineteenth century senior Liberals and Tories would annually board rival barges and travel down the Thames for such a dinner. They must have marvelled at the cargo boats bringing wealth from the four corners of the Empire. Today the view is still impressive, but the cargo boats have been replaced by modern clippers taking tourists and commuters from the O2 to the London Eye.

Close to the Greenwich's World Heritage site, the pub was built on the site of the George Inn in 1837. In 1915 it became the Royal Alfred Aged Merchant Seamen's Institute and became a pub again in 1965 when it was painstakingly restored. Take a sip of the appropriately named Nelson's Bitter, enjoy a plate of the famed whitebait and imagine the happiness of John Rokesmith, who not only married his true love Bella but had his inheritance returned to him. Whoops, I've given away the ending.

The Yacht

5-7 Crane Street, Greenwich, SE10 9NP

BEERS: Wells & Young's, Fuller's and Sharps

The Yacht stands on one of London's oldest thoroughfares and offers dramatic views of the Thames

The British have given many things to the world, including universal time. The Greenwich Meridian line runs through The Yacht, which is situated so close to the Trafalgar Tavern it could almost be an annexe to its more illustrious neighbour. The pub is split into two levels with the top bar's high tables and stools offering a dramatic view of the river from the City to the west and the industrial muscle in the east. Opposite, aircraft from London City Airport can be seen climbing into the sky. The food is hearty and the beers well kept and, at times, it is possible to feel the full vitality of the Thames as the tide turns with the waters rising or falling by a massive 7m (23ft). The pub is used by locals and it is not uncommon to hear a south-east London accent with a full glottal stop.

The Greenwich Meridian, or longitude zero, marks the starting point of every time zone in the world. In the 1840s a railway standard time was established for the whole of England, Scotland and Wales to replace several local time systems. Having a common time was essential once timetables were developed. All station clocks now displayed the same time, which was set by the Royal Observatory in Greenwich. At first the time was transmitted manually by railway staff carrying clocks but the Royal Observatory began transmitting time telegraphically in 1852, and the system was adopted worldwide.

Cutty Sark Tavern

4-7 Ballast Quay, Greenwich, SE10 9PD

BEERS: Young's Bitter and Special plus regular guests.

Over the years, customers looking out of the large upstairs windows of this fine pub must have seen thousands of ships pass by

Visitors arriving by boat to see the *Cutty Sark* can hardly fail to notice its large name emblazoned on its imposing Georgian façade. Built in the early nineteenth century, it is easy to feel the part it has played in the ebb and flow of time. Inside, a large sweeping staircase takes customers up from the downstairs wood-beamed bar to panelled rooms with panoramic views of the new city of London, Canary Wharf and the Millennium Dome. The décor is dark and minimal. In one room hangs an Admiral Robert FitzRoy barometer. He was one of the first men to attempt a scientific weather forecast and he introduced the first daily weather forecasts, which were published in *The Times* in 1860. He also picked Charles Darwin to travel with him on the *Beagle*.

A tavern has stood here from at least the 1740s when it was called the Green Man. At the time it was a common London pub name with possible links to pagan festivals and the celebration of May Day. In 1810 the pub was renamed the Union Tavern, possibly as a mark of support for the union of England and Ireland in 1801. It changed its name again in the 1950s when the famous tea clipper *Cutty Sark* docked in Greenwich. The pub's address gives away the prevailing business of the area; empty cargo vessels returning home would dock to fill up with ballast before heading out to the open seas.

Nearby, on the Thames Path heading back towards Greenwich, is the attractive Trinity Hospital, the oldest building (1613) in Greenwich town centre. Set in the wall is a modern curiosity, a series of small three-dimensional murals called 'Thames Tale' by Amanda Hinge. The whimsy follows Stan and his dog along the Thames path. A children's delight. it baffles most adults even before they've had a beer in the Cutty Sark.

The Pilot Inn

68 River Way, Greenwich, SE10 0BE

BEERS: Fuller's range

A lovely old pub which narrowly escaped demolition when the area was being redeveloped

The Pilot stands in stark contrast to the modernity of the nearby O2, once known as the Millennium Dome. The pub offers a small taste of nineteenth-century Greenwich and is now one of the oldest buildings on the North Greenwich Peninsula. It is now owned by London brewer Fuller's.

The company, food and beer are all good. Inside, it is split over two levels. Outside, there is a spacious and well-turned-out beer garden – the perfect place to enjoy a pint of Fuller's Chiswick bitter.

The pub also has 10 bedrooms, and as it is close to the O2 Clipper stop and the fast boats to Greenwich and central London, it offers a preferable experience to the anonymity of a large hotel.

The Millennium Dome first opened on the night of 31 January 2000. It is the largest space of its kind in the world and is more than 1km (0.6 miles) in circumference and covers over 80,000sq m (861,112sq ft). Built to house the ill-fated Millennium Experience, it was originally described as a celebratory, iconic, non-hierarchical structure offering a vast, flexible space. It was meant to be the centrepiece of the future development of the entire Greenwich Peninsula but closed before the new millennium officially began on 1 January 2001. It stood derelict and painfully quiet until 2007 when it reopened as the O2 music venue.

Anchor & Hope

Riverside, Charlton SE7 7SS

BEERS: Fuller's and Sharps

A friendly local pub with few airs and graces – its outside seating area offers some great views of the Thames Barrier

This is industrial London, the London of builders' yards and recycling plants, the London of barges carrying the city's waste. And here's a locals' pub along this sometimes derelict and downbeat part of the river. The pub was probably built at the end of the nineteenth century, and its turret and cupola hint that it might once have been grander but bomb damage in World War II destroyed much of the building. Inside, it is smart with few airs and graces, and there's a small stage for karaoke and music nights.

From the pub's terrace the front line in the defence against London flooding can be seen. The imposing Thames Barrier is described as one of the engineering wonders of the world, protecting 125sq km (48sq miles) of central London from flood tides surging up Gallions Reach. The barrier was built to prevent a repeat of the devastation caused in 1953 when high tides and a storm combined to create a 3.2m (10.5ft) high surge, killing 307 people across the UK and threatening much of the capital. With its towering stainless-steel piers it spans 520m (1,706ft) across the Thames. The barrier was commissioned in 1984 and has 10 steel gates that can be raised when necessary.

The barrier's four main gates are each as high as a five-storey building and as wide – 61m (200ft) – as the opening section of Tower Bridge. The gates are tested once a month and are best seen from one of the many tour boats. The barrier was originally built to withstand a 1 in 1,000 year flooding, up to the year 2030. However engineers now say that, with continued maintenance, the barrier will provide protection until 2070.

TOWER BRIDGE NORTHSIDE

This part of the river has a strong and varied history. Once there were pastures and hunting grounds for kings. Later, the region became famous for its thriving docklands that eventually fell into disrepair but, today, there is a great sense of energy as new London dominates the skyline with towering white temples to commerce. Look hard enough, though, and you'll still find traces and echoes of the past, with both old and modern London part of the extraordinary jigsaw that makes the capital one of the most dynamic and vibrant cities in the world.

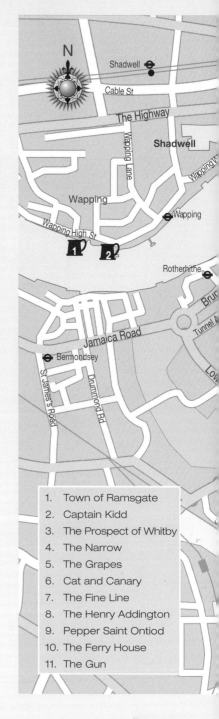

1. Town of Ramsgate
2. Captain Kidd
3. The Prospect of Whitby
4. The Narrow
5. The Grapes
6. Cat and Canary
7. The Fine Line
8. The Henry Addington
9. Pepper Saint Ontiod
10. The Ferry House
11. The Gun

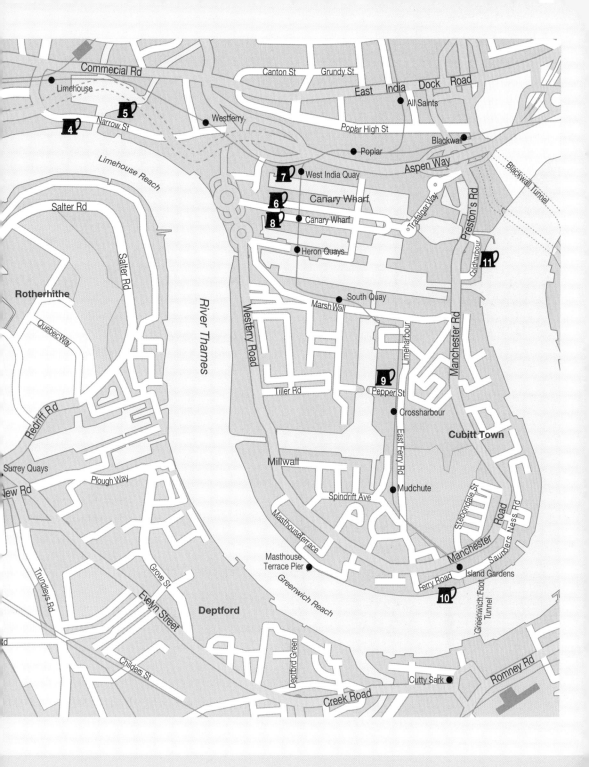

Town of Ramsgate

62 Wapping High Street, Wapping E1W 2PN

BEERS: various

If you like good ale then this small, intimate pub is a winner – a small garden offers fine views of the Thames

At times the small exterior of this Grade II pub looks overwhelmed by its towering neighbours. But inside the small frontage is a long, narrow, wood-panelled pub, built in the 1600s, which is steeped in history. There was a time when fishermen from Ramsgate in Kent would sell their catch from the foot of the adjacent steps, known as Wapping Old Stairs, that lead from the street to the river's edge. Hence the pub's name, but in another era it was called the Red Cow after a flame-haired beauty who served behind the bar. Later it became the Prince of Denmark to attract Danish sailors berthed nearby, showing that even in the seventeenth century there were themed pubs.

The area has some grim associations. Old Stairs was where 'Hanging' Judge Jefferies, fleeing the revolt that overthrew James II in 1688, was caught. He became known as the 'Hanging Judge' because of the punishments he handed out at the trials of the Duke of Monmouth's supporters. Jeffreys was placed in the Tower of London for his own safety and died there the following year, aged 44, of kidney disease. Also, the pub's cellars once held men being press-ganged into serving in the navy and convicts waiting to be sent to Australia. And nearby is Execution Dock where, after the condemned were hanged, their corpses were left to be covered by at least three tides before they were buried. Captain Kidd was executed here in 1701. He's remembered as a notorious pirate but was actually a privateer fighting the French. His crime was not to share the booty with his aristocratic patrons and they got their revenge. As a warning to others, his body was gibbeted and put in a cage by the entrance to the Thames where it stood for 20 years. A painting of William Bligh, the captain of the mutinous *HMS Bounty*, which sailed to Tahiti in 1789, hangs in the bar. Legend has it that Bligh used to drink with the mutineers' leader Fletcher Christian before they set off on their fateful journey.

Captain Kidd

108 Wapping High Street, Wapping, E1W 2NE

BEERS: Samuel Smith's

The pub might not look much from the outside but inside it is a gem with good beer and some fine views of the river

The outside of the pub doesn't promise much. It's a converted warehouse pub with an exterior looking more like a place for storing coffee and fruit imported from the other side of the world than a place to drink a beer and enjoy views of the Thames. Situated close to the site of the Execution Dock, where Captain Kidd was hanged in 1701 for piracy and murder, it only became a pub in the late 1980s and its name is no more than a homage to Kidd because he had no connection with the building.

Like many Samuel Smith pubs, the interior has a smart austerity but with a joke hangman's noose by the door. If you like keenly priced beer, good food (there is a fine restaurant upstairs called the Gallows) and the closeness of the river, which laps right up to the wall of the pub, don't miss it. At times you feel the whole pub is about to cast off, rocking and rolling on the high seas.

From the pub's terrace you can see the moorings of London's river police. The force was founded in 1798 to combat the piracy and pilfering that was endemic on the river. Looting from ships anchored in the Pool of London and the lower reaches of the river was rife, and cost rich merchants hundreds of thousands of pounds a year. This was nearly 30 years before the founding of a force to police the streets of London. It wasn't until 1829 that Home Secretary Sir Robert Peel managed to get the Metropolitan Police Bill through Parliament. Before that London's streets were policed either by watchmen who were seen as bungling, inept and corrupt, or the Bow Street Runners, founded in 1749 by the author Henry Fielding.

The Prospect of Whitby

57 Wapping Wall, Wapping, E1W 3SH

BEERS: five regular beers, including brews from Hop Stuff and Truman's

The Prospect of Whitby is one of London's oldest pubs and its flagstone floor and pewter counter make it a favourite with tourists

The Prospect of Whitby is one of the oldest riverside pubs in London, dating from around 1520. Pub names are derived from many sources, often the names of kings and queens or heraldic imagery, jobs and guilds being commonplace. But there cannot be many pubs whose name comes from a coal supply ship, registered on the River Tyne, that used to berth close by.

In its time the pub has had other names including the Devil and Pelican before acquiring its current name when it was rebuilt after a fire in 1777. Little remains of the original building save for a stone flagged floor in one of the bars, which has an unusual counter made from old oak beer barrels with a pewter top. The explorer Sir Hugh Willoughby sailed from here in 1533 in an ill-starred attempt to discover the north-east passage to China. In the seventeenth century 'Hanging' Judge Jeffreys, the scourge of the Monmouth Rebellion, drank here, and a noose hangs by a window to commemorate the judge's favourite mode of punishment. Samuel Pepys was also a frequent visitor, and besides being a famous diarist was appointed Secretary for the Affairs of the Admiralty by Charles II. A coastal chart presented to him in 1686 is displayed in the upstairs Pepys Room. Charles Dickens is also said to have drunk here.

Outside there is a garden and a small terrace offering wide views of the Thames that are said to have inspired Turner and Whistler. On the opposite side of the road is Wapping Hydraulic Power Station, now an arts centre and restaurant. The power station was built in 1890, and housed six steam boilers and their pumping engines. It provided hydraulic power for the surrounding docks, the bascule Tower Bridge and also for the revolving stages at the London Palladium and Coliseum theatres as well as numerous lifts in City offices and West End department stores.

PROSPECT
OF WHITBY
LONDON'S
OLDEST RIVERSIDE
INN

THE
PROSPECT
OF
WHITBY

LONDON'S
OLDEST
RIVERSIDE
INN

Circa 1520

7481 1095

THE PROSPECT OF WHITBY

The Narrow

44 Narrow Street, Limehouse, E14 8DP

BEERS: Adnams and Fuller's

The Narrow is a delightful Grade II-listed Edwardian building. Once the home of a dock master, it now offers some fine food

The Limehouse area is where the Grand Union Canal and the Regent's Canal meet the Thames, and it is here that the glitz and glamour of celebrity chef Gordon Ramsay meets the traditions of an English public house.

The Narrow was constructed as a dock master's house and became a pub called the Barley Mow, serving Taylor Walker beers. Customers can sit on the large terrace and enjoy the views or experience the relaxed décor of the bar inside from an armchair by the fire. In the back is the Gordon Ramsay dining room, though customers can eat in the bar. There's a simple menu that includes beer-battered fish, hand-cut chips, and mushy peas and braised lentils with spring greens and baby turnip.

Many customers come by train to the nearby Limehouse station. After a beer or two try a walk along the Thames path across the mouth of Limekiln Dock, over a dramatic footbridge with its great views along the rear of the converted warehouses lining the tidal inlet.

The area first became well known in the fourteenth century for its lime kilns. Lime was brought from Kent to serve the building industry, and lime burning was the first of London's air-polluting industries sited downwind of the city. In 1661 Samuel Pepys records that porcelain was made here, while shipbuilding prospered in the area from the sixteenth to the nineteenth centuries. It was also the site of London's first China Town, before it moved to Soho. In the 1830s one of London great brewers, Taylor, began brewing here before it was subsumed in 1960 into the now long-gone Ind Coope.

The Grapes

76 Narrow Street, Limehouse, E14 8BP

BEERS: includes Marston's Pedigree and Timothy Taylor Landlord

For many people The Grapes is a proper pub with bare wooden floorboards, tables and chairs

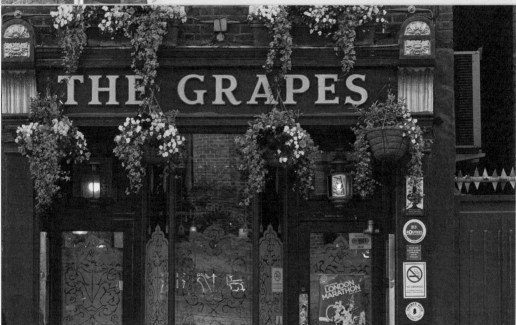

This is a foodies' pub with a fine, if tiny, restaurant upstairs offering the best of each day's catch with more items for meat eaters and vegetarians. Alternatively try the intimate downstairs bar for a roast or fish and chips, accompanied by a pint of Pedigree or Landlord.

The Grapes was built in 1720, backs on to the river and forms part of a rare Georgian brick terrace, giving a fine impression of the scale of riverside development in Limehouse in the eighteenth century. Its interior is the quintessential English pub with bare floorboards, a collection of well-used settles, chairs and tables, and walls adorned with a collection of old prints, plates and curios. At the back there is a small but impressive wooden veranda overlooking the river, from which drinkers can really see the power of the Thames. The pub is probably the inspiration for the Six Jolly Fellowship Porters pub in Charles Dickens' novel *Our Mutual Friend*, where it is described as a tavern of 'dropsical appearance ... long settled down into a state of hale infirmity ...' Some might find it has changed little since Dickens drank here. Opposite The Grapes stands a former pub, known as The House They Left Behind because it was the only building in a Victorian terrace not to be demolished.

Cat and Canary

25-27 Fisherman's Walk, Canary Wharf, E14 4DH

BEERS: full range of Fuller's beers

A vibrant pub, which offers some good beers and fine views over North Dock

Canary Wharf bustles with the energy of commerce, and this attractive, traditional-looking pub is popular with the area's many office workers. It stands right on the water's edge of North Dock and overlooks cranes, which have stood silent since the dock shut in 1960.

Inside, the pub looks as if it has been here for generations, but it is relatively new. It is just one small part of the massive development that is still going on, transforming this part of London into a vibrant financial and retail hub. The décor has lots of wood and brass, space for large groups to stand and tables for those who prefer to sit. It has the reputation for being a pub to watch sport, and several large TV monitors are placed strategically around the bar. Outside, there is a large terrace,

which is popular with large groups on warm sunny evenings. Sometimes it can be quite noisy and boisterous, but that is part of its friendly charm.

Once a year, runners taking part in the London Marathon pass close by. Some of the best views of this great human spectacle are nearby when thousands of people - from speeding elite runners at the front to plodders at the rear - attempt to run more than 42km (26 miles). The excellent transport links to Canary Wharf make it a popular spot for spectators before the runners head to the finish in St James's Park.

The beer range includes Fuller's Frontier lager. Bright and golden, it has distinctive notes of citrus fruits and melon that harmonise with the soft biscuit flavours of the malt.

The Fine Line

29-30 Fisherman's Walk, Canary Wharf, E14 4DH

BEERS: Fuller's

The Fine Line is very popular with office workers wanting a drink and a quick bite to eat after a hard day's work

The Fine Line at Canary Wharf is a lively bar, right on the riverside. It is one of a chain owned by west London brewer, Fuller's. There's a quiet opulence with stylish leather and a colour scheme of rich reds and blacks. Most customers drink outside or downstairs in the large bar, while two sweeping staircases take people upstairs to a balcony bar, ideal for those wanting a more discreet assignation. As befits a bar primarily for well-heeled suits, the drinks range is wide and eclectic with expensive bottles of champagne and Fuller's London Pride. The menu includes a range of contemporary English dishes augmented by European dishes for the office workers who pop in

for lunch. Highlights include ale pies, steaks and platters with olives, hummus and spicy sausages.

Not many tourists venture to this part of London, but they are missing out because Canary Wharf is a thriving, vibrant business district. Until 50 years ago Canary Wharf was a giant cargo warehouse at the centre of West India Docks. When London ceased being an important shipping port because the new giant cargo carriers could not navigate upriver and instead berthed at Tilbury and Felixstowe, its future looked bleak. The rusting cranes fell silent. Now it is now home to three of the country's tallest buildings: Canary Wharf Tower, 8 Canada Square and Citigroup Centre.

The Henry Addington

22-28 Mackenzie Walk, Canary Wharf, E14 4PH

BEERS: good range of British ales and world beers

A smart busy pub close to the shops and offices of Canary Wharf

Financial sharks might walk outside this pub, but Canary Wharf has now become one of the hottest spots in London for seal watching. According to the Zoological Society of London, the water in the Thames has improved so much in recent years that these marine mammals are now frequent visitors.

The Henry Addington has a long, stylish, brown bar, and there are several tables outside on the pavement. It also offers a great view of the full majesty of the Shard in Southwark. A skyscraper, it stands 310m high and for the moment is not only London's but Europe's tallest building.

The pub is named after a former Prime Minister who held the top job for three years from 1801 during the reign of George III. A doctor as well as a politician, he is said to have enjoyed royal favour as he treated the King during one of his periods of mental illness.

A wide range of ever-changing ales is served, but permanently on the bar is its own Nicholson's Pale Ale, which has been brewed by Cornish brewer St Austell. Easy drinking, it's become the best-selling ale across the Nicholson's estate of 70 plus pubs. Made with Cornish malt, it is infused with a heady citrus cocktail of English and European hops.

Pepper Saint Ontiod

21 Pepper Street, Millwall, E14 9RP

BEERS: cask beers

A modern pub located in the heart of Docklands – it offers football on big screens, quizzes and music nights

Heard about Saint Ontiod? Of course not. Ontiod is an acronym meaning On the Isle of Dogs. It's a fun place, 'a proper pub with pork scratchings' says the owner. Previously called the Puzzle, the pub is owned by the same company that operates the Tooting Tram & Social and the Balham Bowls Club. It is located at the heart of the Isle of Dogs, near Crossharbour DLR Station on the stunning Millwall Inner Dock, just a few minutes south from Canary Wharf; to the west is the London Sailing School and some of London's most striking views.

The owner likes creating quirky, local pubs. Inside you'll find a large, spacious, modern ground-floor bar that teems with vintage lampshades, plush sofas and classic furniture. Upstairs there is a games room and a big screen for showing football matches, and outside a good drinking area. The food includes burgers, fish and chips, sandwiches and pizzas. Film fans might recognize the outside Millwall dock because it was the location for the boat stunts in the James Bond film *The World is Not Enough* that was made in 1999.

The Ferry House

26 Ferry Street, Isle of Dogs E14 3DT

BEERS: Courage Best Bitter and Young's Bitter

A well-loved pub, which has seen many changes over the years

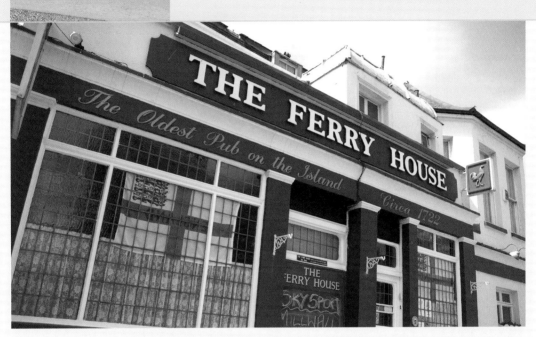

Recently refurbished, this is probably the oldest pub on the Isle of Dogs. The current building dates from 1822 and was built to house the ferrymen who took people to Greenwich. It features a cosy main bar, a dining room, function room and a small beer garden. Its location is ideal for anyone walking along the Thames Path. Situated at the foot of the Isle of Dogs, the pub is just a short walk from Greenwich Foot Tunnel, which opened in 1902 and put an end to the ferry.

Years ago, the riverside at the Ferry, with its view over to the splendour of Greenwich, must have buzzed with activity as a pageant of ships passed by. Barges laden with fish would hurry upstream to Billingsgate. Coal carriers headed towards gas works and power stations. Rusty freighters with precious fruit from warmer climes steamed by. But with the demise of the speeding clippers, such as *Cutty Sark*, named after the beautiful witch in the Robert Burns 'Tam O'Shanter', the Thames sailing barges now catch the eye. There can be few better sights than such a barge with its tanned mainsail, tacking up to Tower Bridge against the last of the ebb of the tide.

The Gun

27 Coldharbour, Isle of Dogs, E14 9NS

BEERS: Adnams and Sambrooks

A fine pub, which has survived many changes – it now has a fine food menu and is a firm favourite

The Gun is a survivor – despite massive redevelopment of the area, a fire that devastated it in 2001 and the bombs of World War II, it still thrives. In fact the pub – easily accessible from Canary Wharf by taxi, tube or bus – is a docklands jewel with stunning views from its pretty terrace to the O2 arena. It is frequently used by concert-goers before and after a show.

Once, the pub's customers were workers from the local foundry or wharfs, and for many years it was a down-at-heel pub with few airs and graces. But the area has changed and the dockworkers are now long gone. Today it's a smart gastropub serving modern British cuisine. Diners in the restaurant can look forward to Lindisfarne rock oysters and roast saddle of salt-marsh-reared Welsh lamb. In summer a Portuguese barbecue, known as a grelha, is fired into life serving sardines, grilled chorizo and cataplana – a fish and seafood stew slowly cooked in a copper cataplana dish – big favourites. The pub menu includes upmarket fish-finger sandwiches and Welsh rarebit.

A Grade II listed building, it was meticulously restored after the fire in 2001 and now has chic décor and stunning murals. The pub dates back to the early eighteenth century and has open fires and two private dining rooms, one of which, the River Room, is apparently where Lord Horatio Nelson used to meet Lady Emma Hamilton. The Sea Lord, who died at the Battle of Trafalgar in 1805, had a house nearby and regularly visited the docks to inspect the guns being cast in the foundry. The pub also has links with smugglers who are said to have landed contraband nearby, and inside there is a hidden tunnel and a spy hole in a secret, circular tunnel for trying to avoid the excise men.

CANALSIDE/ RIVER LEA

The Victorians often get a bad press but they knew how to build things that lasted, and they created the waterways that made the transportation of building materials and produce into London much easier. They used Regent's Canal, which travels past two of London's great green lungs, Regent's Park and London Zoo. It joins the Grand Union Canal, which runs from Paddington west towards Brentford. The River Lea, which ends at the heart of London's Olympic village, is not a canal in the true sense but a river that has been harnessed and controlled. The paths that run beside all these waterways offer some of the finest views of London, and a marvellous place to sample some of the capital's best pubs and beers.

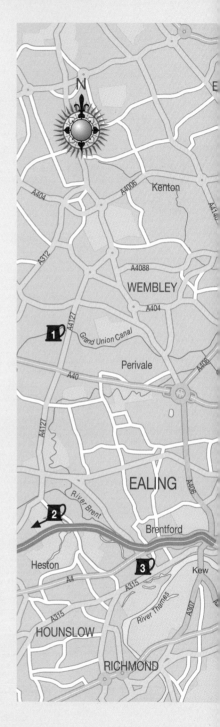

1. The Black Horse
2. The General Eliott
3. The Weir, Brentford
4. Grand Junction Arms
5. Union Tavern
6. The Bridge House
7. The Warwick Castle
8. Union Bar and Grill
9. Lockside
10. The Constitution
11. Rotunda
12. The Palm Tree
13. The Crown
14. Princess of Wales
15. Ferry Boat Inn

The Black Horse

425 Oldfield Lane North, Greenford, UB6 0AS

BEERS: Fuller's

The Black Horse is a handy stopping-off point for anyone walking or cycling along the tow path

The garden is large with plenty of outside seating offering a leafy view over the Grand Union Canal. This is a quiet rest stop for anyone walking or cycling along the towpath. Craft cruising on the canal will often moor here. Various sports, including football, are shown on the TV screens but, as the pub is split into several levels, there is plenty of room for those who do not want to watch. There are regular poker nights, a quiz night and 'open mike'

jam sessions. The pub's menu is traditional with very popular grill nights.

The garden is large and craft cruising on the Grand Union Canal will often moor here. The canal wasn't built as a result of a single vision but was created in the 1920s when several different waterways merged. More than 210km (130 miles) long, it takes in the centre of London, the Chiltern Hills and the industrial suburbs of Birmingham.

The General Eliott

St Johns Road, Uxbridge UB8 2UR

BEERS: range of cask ales

Well-loved local pub with a canal-side garden, which is the perfect place for a relaxing beer and a barbecue on a summer's day

General Eliott was best known for commanding the defence of Gibraltar against the Spanish 1779-83, which nearly saw his force starved to death. The pub that bears his name is best known for the excellence of its garden right on the Grand Union Canal's bank, and with a traditional pub menu customers are unlikely to starve.

A popular local, the pub is often used by coarse fisherman after a day in pursuit of the roach, perch, bream, chub, pike and carp which live in the canal. Inside, the pub has one large single bar, it is friendly and seems at its intimate best when the lights are dimmed and there is live, local music.

Just before Uxbridge is Cowley Peachey junction, it is here the canal begins to rise through up the River Colne valley. Outside the pub there are some moorings, which prove to be very popular in the summer.

Between 1798 and 1805 the Grand Junction Canal was opened, which greatly increased the trade through Uxbridge. The canal was London's principal link with the rest of the UK's canal system. At the start of the nineteenth century a popular passenger boat, the Paddington Packet boat, ran between the inland port of Paddington and Uxbridge.

The Weir operates
a smart dress
policy
Thank...

The Weir

24 Market Place, Brentford, TW8 9RB

BEERS: Fuller's London Pride, Erdinger Wheat Beer and a range of Belgian bottled beers

A foodie's delight, the garden of this historic pub runs down to the edge of the Grand Union Canal

The Weir is a gastropub with its large garden running down to the edge of the Grand Union Canal. Gastropubs are said to be like French brasseries and were created by Michael Belben who, in 1991, opened the Eagle in London's Farringdon Road with his business partner and chef, David Eyre. Where the Eagle went, others followed. The Weir's menu is constantly changing but signature dishes include: pan-fried duck breast and Chateaubriand served on a hot, chicken liver parfait with a sweet onion marmalade and Melba toast; crayfish, crab and chilli tagliatelle; and risotto with wild mushroom, sweet black garlic and rocket.

Brentford is an old, historical town and the place where two rivers and a canal meet. It was once one of the most important towns in Middlesex, and dates from the late first century AD. It grew in importance through the Middle Ages as traffic on the road out of London increased, providing a stop-off point for refreshment and stabling. The pub was formerly the White Horse, and is probably the oldest pub in Brentford having been licensed in 1603. There was a house on this site where the artist J.M.W. Turner stayed as a child with his uncle, and expressed an interest in painting, so starting his fascination with the colour of light and water.

Grand Junction Arms

Acton Lane, Willesden, NW10 7AD

BEERS: Wells & Young's

A large Victorian pub, it features good Young's beer, regular jazz nights and is a pleasant place to relax

A real pub serving great beers with a gorgeous garden beside the Grand Union Canal. It is an oasis in the heart of Park Royal. Situated close to Harlesden Station, it is a somewhat faded Victorian pub built on three floors. Outside there is a part-decked area that overlooks the canal. Inside there is a traditional public bar, a small snug and a large barn-style rear bar that leads out on to the patio with steps leading down to the benches on the canal path.

Park Royal is one of London's industrial areas and home to the Guinness Brewery where brewing began in 1937. Until a few years ago most of the Guinness drunk in Britain came from this site, which has now been demolished. Now the dry stout drunk in the UK comes from the Arthur Guinness brewery at St James's Gate, Dublin. Guinness is based on the Porter style that originated in London in the early eighteenth century, and is one of the most successful beer brands worldwide. A distinctive feature is the burnt, roasted barley taste.

Guinness is well known for its strong marketing, which began in 1928 when the company appointed the advertising agency S.H. Benson and began a pilot scheme in Scotland. The agency came up with the slogan 'Guinness is Good For You'. Within two years it was a national campaign and thousands of doctors were being approached with the idea that Guinness was good for insomnia, nerves, digestion and tiredness. It was even prescribed to women with anaemia. Today's advertising rules outlaw such claims.

Union Tavern

45 Woodfield Road, Maida Vale, W9 2BA

BEERS: good range of beers from some of London's newer breweries

Union Tavern is a fine example of a vibrant pub opened in the middle of the nineteenth century – a boom time for pub building

Built while Queen Victoria was on the throne, Union Tavern has been tastefully remodelled over the years while remaining true to itself. The Victorian era was one of great expansion for the pub and brewing industry as people began to have more free time and greater disposable income. The smarter entrepreneurs built pubs near new developments, such as canals, and close to bridges to maximize the number of customers. In the early Victorian era the pubs would not have looked very different from the houses that they were built next to. But by the beer boom of the 1860s and 1870s, when Britain's industrial workforce wanted beer to slake its collective thirst, the pubs' design became increasingly distinct and vibrant. They had to stand out and be more comfortable than people's homes.

Union Tavern is a two-floored pub, the main bar being split into a drinking and a smart dining area. From the snug lower bar, reached by a spiral staircase, there is access to a canal-side garden, the jewel in the pub's crown. The terrace draws people like a magnet to this part of Westbourne Park and it can get very busy outside, especially on a summer's day, and while finding a seat can be difficult it is possible to book a table. The view across the canal to the bus depot might not be the greatest, but that does not detract from the lure of the water. The food is modern English pub food, including excellent pies with a variety of fillings, plus exotic dishes. Many people come for the shared platters. The Sunday roasts are popular and in summer there is a barbecue.

The Bridge House

13 Westbourne Terrace Road, Little Venice, W2 6NG

BEERS: Sharp's Doom Bar and Timothy Taylor's Landlord plus two guest beers

There is a touch of glamour to this pub, which is also home to the Canal Café Theatre

Situated close to Warwick Avenue underground station, the Bridge House is at the heart of Little Venice where the Paddington arm of the Grand Union Canal meets Regent's Canal. The area is home to many of London's boat people, whose craft are moored nearby. The use of the name Little Venice is attributed to the poet Robert Browning, who died in Venice in 1899 and was buried in Poets' Corner in Westminster Abbey.

This section of the canal is excellent for towpath walkers and the 4km (2.5 mile) route to the glamour and clamour of Camden Market, and takes in many fine houses and buildings as it goes past Regent's Park and London Zoo. Canal-boat trips pick up and drop off passengers very close to the pub. It was built at the beginning of the nineteenth century in a graceful neo-classical style and exudes an air of bohemian opulence. The lighting is subdued and the furniture a mix of sofas, and tables and chairs of different sizes. In keeping with the artistic atmosphere, red velvet curtains conceal the theatre doors. Given its prime location in a stylish part of London, it can get busy both inside and outside.

Beers include ales from Adnams, Greene King and Fuller's, as well as a range of specialist continental lagers. The menu has traditional English sausage and mash, steaks and plenty of salads. On the first floor is the Canal Café Theatre – a fringe comedy theatre – that has been holding a weekly news-review show for the last 30 years. According to the *Guinness Book of Records* it is the longest-running comedy show in the world. There's more comedy and plays through the week. Have a meal downstairs before a show and afterwards pop down for a drink.

The Warwick Castle

6 Warwick Place, Maida Vale, W9 2PX

BEERS: Greene King beer plus regular guests

A village pub, close to the heart of London

This no-nonsense pub exudes the atmosphere of a well-run village local. From the flower displays outside and the large open windows to the smart, relaxed interior, most things at the Warwick exude class. The pub gets its name, as does the street, from the original landowner who married Jane Warwick of Warwick Hall, near Carlisle, in 1778. Several local streets were also named for her in the mid-nineteenth century.

The pub is a great example of Victorian design and retains many of its original features. The Grade II-listed building dates from 1846 and has a dark green frontage that blends in with the rest of the terrace, which is why it features in the Campaign for Real Ale's London Regional Inventory of Pub Interiors. It still has some of its original windows. Inside, there are three drinking rooms and a small snug with an elegant marbled fireplace. The food is good, but there is no obligation to sit down and eat. Boot-wearing dog walkers who want to settle down with a newspaper and a pint are warmly welcomed. There's also a wide range of cask Greene King beers, including a house ale called Boater's Brew.

Union Bar and Grill

4 Sheldon Square, Paddington, W2 6EZ

BEERS: regular guest ales and a range of lagers

A bustling, modern venue that is close to Paddington Station and is well used by office workers

For decades most of London's canal sides stood abandoned, being watery wastelands that bore the scars of a former industrial life. But many have been bought back to life, such as Sheldon Square, close to Paddington Station and Warwick Avenue underground, which forms part of a new waterside development and is right by the side of the Union Bar and Grill. It is a modern venue with large panels of glass giving good views on to the water.

The interior is reminiscent of a hi-tech factory with lots of shiny floor space and wooden tables, chairs and stools. Outside there is a large jumbo umbrella and seating for those who want to watch canal boats pass by or lycra-clad cyclists on the walkway. The food is fairly typical of a gastro bar.

There are burgers and English dishes with Italian pastas, Spanish meats and a selection of oriental dishes including Thai curries. It gets busy after 5pm when workers leave their offices and have an early evening drink before heading home.

The Paddington basin forms the end of the Grand Union canal. It is the last part of a 20km (13 mile) lock-free stretch of canal that was opened in 1801 to bring coal and building materials to the centre of London. When it was drained in 2003 for repair as part of the development process, more than 24,000 fish were rescued, including carp, eels, bream and perch. The canal no longer brings goods into the city, but its walkways are a great way to get an unexpected glimpse of the new London.

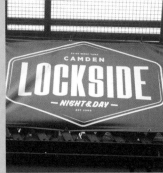

Lockside

75-89 Upper Walkway, Camden Lock Place, NW1 8AF

BEERS: wide selection of bottled beers including the Adnams range

The Lockside décor might be minimalist but it is the perfect place for anyone looking for a party

On a summer's night the whole of Camden Lock seems to rock like one great party. It is a place of frenetic energy and youthful non-conformity. There are many bars pounding out all kinds of music. The Dingwalls complex, home to a comedy club, is a big attraction though musically nothing quite matches the time when Elvis Costello and friends would just turn up and do a gig.

The Ice Wharf, owned by J.D. Wetherspoon and just off Camden Road, is a no-nonsense introduction to the area. It's a perfect place to meet, but where next? Lockside might not look that good with its minimalist interior and eclectic mix of chairs and sofas that never seem to be in the same place twice. On some days it is fine for a quiet lunch but, in the evenings, it vibrates to the sound of DJs spinning their decks. Outside there is decking and picnic tables, and the best view of Camden Lock. Arrive early on sunny days to get a table.

The food won't win any Michelin awards but it's absolutely fine – nachos with cheese vie for attention with *bruschetta* served with goat's cheese and burgers. And if the sun is out, try the barbecue on the veranda. The beer list offers some surprises, including a Belgium classic Chimay Blue and the Czech Budvar. If you want to dance, go inside for some of London's best DJs or just sit outside and watch the sun set.

The Constitution

42 St Pancras Way, Camden, NW1 0QT

BEERS: range of cask ales

A traditional pub close to Camden Market, it is a popular place for people to unwind and relax

The pub's large outdoor area, by the canal side, makes it a popular venue. It is especially busy in summer when burgers are served from the barbecue. Inside, the pub is split into two floors; the downstairs area is smaller and more atmospheric and people go upstairs to play pool.

The nearby Camden Market has now become a vibrant tourist attraction. In 1972 three former warehouses were used as craft workshops and, soon after, a small craft market opened in a cobbled yard at the weekends. It quickly became a success, especially as the stalls could open on Sundays when most shops were then closed. The novelty of shopping on a Sunday, and the slightly risqué and Bohemian air of Camden attracted the likes of students, radicals and musicians. By 1985 other markets had opened in the streets nearby and, since then, Camden Market has continued to grow and you can now buy just about anything here. The weekends are still the best time to visit because that's when Camden Lock Village is open. The fashion market at the Electric Ballroom opens on Sunday only. Most people take the tube to Camden Town or Chalk Farm underground station.

Rotunda

Kings Place, 90 York Way, King's Cross, N1 9AG

BEERS: range of draught and bottled beers

A smart bar which is part of a larger arts and leisure complex – it offers some fine views of the canal boats in the Battlebridge Basin

Pubs and bars next to water come in many forms, but there cannot be many as dramatic as the Rotunda in the Kings Place office and cultural centre. It is a relaxing haven close to the bustling chaos of King's Cross in north London. The bar and restaurant is a curvaceous canalside venue with a relaxing terrace, which follows the bow of the glass-fronted building along Regent's Canal and Battlebridge Basin. It has a modern interior with more sweeping curves, lots of dark wood, blue furniture and abundant light.

The menu includes a starter of smoked eel with pressed beetroot and horseradish. Beef and lamb are sourced from the owner's own farm in Northumberland and are matured on the premises. Jazz is played in the atrium every Friday, while the patio is a perfect place to watch the moored barges bobbing in the water while enjoying a beer. The thriving basin is home to 17 residential narrow boats and also hosts a wide variety of bird, animal, fish and plant life.

The basin is one of the larger basins on Regent's Canal. It opened in 1822 and was used for one of London's most unusual imports, ice from Norway, that was used to make ice cream and for other purposes. The former ice warehouse, built in 1862, is now the London Canal Museum. The building was built by Carlo Gatti, a famous ice cream maker and inside there is still a Victorian ice well. The museum tells the story of London's canals. Visitors can explore the inside of a narrow-boat cabin, and look at the canal-themed art and cargo equipment.

The Palm Tree

Grove Road, Mile End, E3 5BH

BEERS: various cask ales

A friendly pub used by people of all ages – the regular music nights are always well attended

There is something old-fashioned about this atmospheric East End pub by the canal in Mile End Park. Sit inside one of its two rooms with a pint of ale and it is possible to imagine it in its heyday, but stay long enough and you will discover that the East End is still alive as locals pack in for live jazz and good fun. The décor is muted thanks to the slightly faded carpets and well-used wooden furniture, while the walls are decorated with pictures of local boxers and performers.

Outside there is an extensive grassy area next to the Regent's Canal that forms the western edge of the park. The park was created in the 1940s as part of a plan to connect parts of London to the Thames. The canal cuts across north London and links the Paddington arm of the Grand Union in the west to the Limehouse basin and Thames in the east. In nearby Copperfield Road is the Ragged School Museum. Housed in a group of three canalside buildings, it once formed the largest ragged (or free) school for London's poor. It was opened by the Irish philanthropist Thomas Barnardo in 1877. The museum was founded in 1990 to tell the history of these schools and the social history of the East End, where thousands of children died of disease and lived in squalor. Barnardo died in 1905, by which time the charity he had founded, which still exists and bears his name, ran 96 homes caring for more than 8,500 children.

The Crown

223 Grove Road, Victoria Park, E3 5SN

BEERS: changing range

A fine-dining pub, it is also a relaxing place to enjoy a pint of real ale

There is something reassuringly welcoming about this fine nineteenth-century building, which stands by Victoria Park and the Hertford Union canal. Inside, it is a smart and trendy gastropub with lots of wooden floors, deep sofas and patches of eccentric wall coverings. Upstairs there are three dining rooms and a fine balcony with commanding views over the park.

Being a gastropub there is an emphasis on wine, but Geronimo (the company that owns the pub) has an excellent reputation for its beers, and frequently features Sharps and Adnams. The background to the pub's ethos is a chef with experience of a Michelin-starred restaurant. Dexter cattle provide the beef. The Dexter is the shortest British cow and comes from south-west Ireland where it certainly dates back to 1845. Some say it is descended from the predominately black cattle of the early Celts. The meat is famed for its flavour and the chefs at the Crown try and use every inch of a Dexter, including the marrow bone. Vegetarians are also catered for.

Opposite is Victoria Park, which stretches across the East End of London, like a giant green lung, and is very much a people's park, the perfect place to stroll after an ample lunch. Its southern boundary is marked by the Hertford Canal, built in 1830. A short canal, it was built to link the Grand Union with the Lee to avoid the tidal waters of the Thames around the long curves of the Isle of Dogs. It is also known as Duckett's Cut after Sir George Duckett who financed its construction.

Princess of Wales

146 Lea Bridge Road, Clapton, E5 9QB

BEERS: Wells & Young's plus a wide range of guest beers from London brewers

A traditional pub where it is possible to enjoy a fine pint of Young's Bitter after a pleasant riverside stroll

Once this large pub by the River Lea was called the Prince of Wales, but it was one of two Young's pubs renamed to commemorate Diana, Princess of Wales after her death in 1997, the other being the Princess of Wales in south Wimbledon. The company's chairman John Young had worked closely with Diana who was patron of the National Hospital for Neurology and Neurosurgery. His royal connections extended to the Queen, who visited Young's when the company celebrated its 150th anniversary in 1981, and the Queen Mother, who famously pulled a pint of Young's Special in a Young's pub. The Prince of Wales and the Earl of Wessex later emulated their grandmother by drawing pints in Young's pubs.

The first mention of a pub on the site was in the 1860s, and it was bought by Young's in 1974 from Whitbread. Once it was very much a locals' pub with piano music and popular songs in the crowded saloon bar. And in an era before most pubs served food there was a stall outside selling East End favourites, such as jellied eels, whelks and winkles. Not surprisingly, due to its riverside location, the pub has long been associated with angling and boating, and in summer people even swam here. Recently refurbished, it is a smart dining pub with a great range of beers. With a pleasant outdoor seating area, it has to be one of the best pubs in East London on a warm, sunny day. There's easy access to Lee Valley Park, which runs either side of the river.

Ferry Boat Inn

Ferry Lane, Tottenham Hale, N17 9NG

BEERS: range of cask-conditioned ales

The Ferry Boat Inn has a fine location and a great beer garden which is perfect for relaxing in on a sunny day

This area by the pub has been an important place for crossing the River Lea (also spelt Lee) for hundreds of years, and the current pub was probably built around 1738. The pub looks every inch a country inn, which makes it unusual for this part of London. It has a flagstone floor, large wood-burning fireplaces and comfortable seating. Outside there is a large beer garden running along the river. There is usually a good range of cask beers and the food menu should suit most tastes.

The cycle and pedestrian path beside the River Lea has to be one of London's great secrets. The route snakes 42km (26 miles) from the Thames in east London to Ware in Hertfordshire. From the Isle of Dogs the route travels through a tapestry of parks, marshland – including the legendary Hackney Marshes, said to hold the world record for the largest number of football pitches (88) in one place – and waterways. The area is now a curious mix of the new Olympic stadium and rusting, abandoned industry where urban sprawl and commerce lie side by side with the wildlife.

For anyone exploring the Lea by foot or cycle, the Ferry boat Inn, which is 8km (5 miles) from Bow as the path goes, offers a welcome place to eat or drink. And being close to Tottenham Hale Station there is a fast route back to the centre of London. The area around the Ferry Boat Inn is a haven for nature lovers. It is close to the Lee Valley Reservoir Chain with its 13 artificial lakes, providing drinking water for London. A tranquil site, consisting of wooded islands and marshes, it is packed with vegetation and wildlife.

Pub addresses and websites

The Albany
Queens Road, Thames Ditton
Surrey, KT7 0QY
www.the-albany.co.uk
TRAIN: Hampton Court

All Bar One (Butler's Wharf)
Shad Thames
Butler's Wharf, SE1 2YG
www.allbarone.co.uk
TUBE: London Bridge

The Anchor
34 Park Street
Bankside, SE1 9EF
TUBE: London Bridge

Anchor & Hope
Riverside
Charlton, SE7 7SS
TRAIN: Charlton

The Anchor Tap
20 Horselydown Lane
Southwark, SE1 2LN
TUBE: Tower Hill

The Angel
101 Bermondsey Wall East
Rotherhithe, SE16 4NB
TUBE: Bermondsey

The Anglers (Teddington)
3 Broom Road, Teddington
Middlesex, TW11 9NR
www.anglers-teddington.co.uk
TRAIN: Teddington

The Anglers (Walton-on-Thames)
Riverside Road, Walton-on-
Thames
Surrey, KY12 4PE
www.anglerswalton.com
TRAIN: Shepperton

The Banker
Cousin Lane
Cannon Street, EC4R 3TE
TUBE: Cannon Street

Barmy Arms
The Embankment, Twickenham
Middlesex, TW1 3DU
TRAIN: Twickenham

The Barrowboy and Banker
6/8 Borough High Street
Southwark, SE1 9QQ
www.barrowboy-and-banker.
co.uk
TUBE: London Bridge

The Bell & Crown
11 Thames Road
Chiswick, W4 3PL
www.bell-and-crown.co.uk
TUBE: Gunnersbury

The Bishop
2 Bishops Hall, Kingston-upon-
Thames
Surrey, KT1 1PY
www.thebishopkingston.co.uk
TRAIN: Kingston-upon-Thames

The Black Friar
174 Queen Victoria Street
Blackfriars, EC4V 4EG
TUBE: Blackfriars/St Pauls

The Black Horse
425 Oldfield Lane North
Greenford, UB6 0AS
www.blackhorsegreenford.co.uk
TUBE: Greenford

The Black Lion
2 South Black Lion Lane
Hammersmith, W6 9TJ
www.theblacklion-hammer-
smith.co.uk
TUBE: Stamford Brook

Blue Anchor
13 Lower Mall
Hammersmith, W6 9DJ
www.blueanchorlondon.com
TUBE: Hammersmith

The Boaters Inn
Canbury Gardens, Lower Ham
Road
Kingston-upon-Thames, KT2
5AU
www.boaterskingston.com
TRAIN: Kingston-upon-Thames

The Boathouse
Brewhouse Lane
Putney, SW15 2JX
www.boathouseputney.co.uk
TUBE: Putney Bridge

The Bricklayer's Arms
32 Watermans Street
Putney, SW15 1DD
www.bricklayers-arms.co.uk
TUBE: Putney Bridge

The Bridge House
13 Westbourne Terrace Road
Little Venice, W2 6NG
www.thebridgehouselittlevenice.
co.uk
TUBE: Warwick Avenue

The Bulls Head (Barnes)
373 Lonsdale Road
Barnes, SW13 9PY
www.geronimo-inns.co.uk/
london-the-bulls-head
TUBE: Barnes Terrace

The Bulls Head (Chiswick)
15 Strand-on-the-Green
Chiswick, W4 3PQ
TUBE: Gunnersbury

Captain Kidd
108 Wapping High St.
Wapping, E1W 2NE
TUBE: Wapping

Cat and Canary
25-27 Fisherman's Walk
Canary Wharf, E14 4DH
www.catandcanary.co.uk
TUBE: Canary Wharf

The Cat's Back
86-88 Point Pleasant
Wandsworth, SW18 1NN
www.thecatsback.com
TUBE: East Putney

The City Barge
27 Strand-on-the-Green
Chiswick, W4 3PH
TUBE: Gunnersbury or Kew

The Constitution
42 St Pancras Way
Camden, NW1 0QT
www.conincamden.com
TUBE: Camden Town

The Crabtree Tavern
Rainville Road
Fulham, W6 9HL
www.thecrabtreew6.co.uk
TUBE: Hammersmith

The Cross Keys
1 Lawrence Street
Chelsea, SW3 5NB
www.thecrosskeyschelsea.
co.uk
TUBE: South Kensington

The Crown
223 Grove Road
Victoria Park, E3 5SN
TUBE: Mile End

Cutty Sark Tavern
4-7 Ballast Quay
Greenwich, SE10 9PD
www.cuttysarkse10.co.uk
TUBE: Cutty Sark

The Dickens Inn
St Katharine's Dock,
Tower Hill, E1W 1UH
www.dickensinn.co.uk
TUBE: Tower Gateway

Doggett's Coat & Badge
1 Blackfriars Bridge
Southwark, SE1 9UD
www.doggettscoatandbadge.
co.uk
TUBE: Southwark

The Dove
19 Upper Mall
Hammersmith, W6 9TA
www.dovehammersmith.co.uk
TUBE: Hammersmith

Duke's Head
8 Lower Richmond Road
Putney, SW15 1JN
www.dukesheadputney.com
TUBE: Putney Bridge

Ferry Boat Inn
Ferry Lane
Tottenham Hale, N17 9NG
www.stonegatepubs.com/ferry-
boat-london
TUBE: Tottenham Hale

The Ferry House
26 Ferry Street
Isle of Dogs, E14 3DT
www.theferryhousepub.co.uk
TUBE: Island Gardens (DLR)

The Fine Line
29-30 Fisherman's Walk
Canary Wharf, E14 4DH
www.finelinecanarywharf.co.uk
TUBE: Canary Wharf

The Flower Pot
Thames Street, Sunbury-on-
Thames
Surrey, TW16 6AA
www.theflowerpotsunbury.co.uk
TRAIN: Sunbury

Founders Arms
52 Hopton Street
Southwark, SE1 9JH
www.foundersarms.co.uk
TUBE: Southwark/St Pauls

The Gazebo
Thames Street, Kingston-upon-
Thames
Surrey, KT1 1PH
TRAIN: Kingston-upon-Thames

The General Eliott
St Johns Road
Uxbridge, UB8 2UR
www.generaleliottuxbridge.co.uk
TUBE: Uxbridge

The Gipsy Moth
60 Greenwich Church Street
Greenwich, SE10 9BL
www.thegipsymothgreenwich.
co.uk
TUBE: Cutty Sark (DLR)

Grand Junction Arms
Acton Lane
Willesden, NW10 7AD
TUBE: Harlesden

The Grapes
76 Narrow Street
Limehouse, E14 8BP
www.thegrapes.co.uk
TUBE: Westferry (DLR)

The Gun
27 Coldharbour
Isle of Dogs, E14 9NS
www.thegundocklands.com
TUBE: Canary Wharf

The Hart's Boatyard
Portsmouth Road, Surbiton
Surrey, KT6 4HL
www.hartsboatyard.co.uk
TRAIN: Surbiton

The Henry Addington
22-28 Mackenzie Walk
Canary Wharf, E14 4P
TUBE: Canary Wharf

The Horniman At Hay's
Hay's Galleria, Counter Street
Southwark, SE1 2HD
TUBE: London Bridge

Kings Arms Hotel
Lion Gate, Hampton Court Road
East Molesey, Surrey, KT8 9DD
www.kingsarmshamptoncourt.
co.uk
TRAIN: Hampton Court

Lockside
75-89 Upper Walkway
Camden Lock Place, NW1 8AF
www.locksidecamden.com
TUBE: Camden Town

The London Apprentice
62 Church Street, Isleworth
Middlesex, TW7 6BG
www.thelondonapprentice.co.uk
TRAIN/TUBE: Richmond

The Magpie
64 Thames Street, Sunbury-on-Thames
Surrey, TW16 6AF
www.magpiesunbury.com
TRAIN: Sunbury

The Market Porter
9 Stoney St., Borough Market
London Bridge, SE1 9AA
www.markettaverns.co.uk
TUBE: London Bridge

The Mawson Arms
110 Chiswick Lane South,
Chiswick, W4 2QA
www.mawsonarmschiswick.co.uk
TUBE: Stamford Brook

The Mayflower
117 Rotherhithe Street
Rotherhithe, SE16 4NF
www.mayflowerpub.co.uk
TUBE: Rotherhithe

The Moby Dick
6 Russell Court East
Rotherhithe, SE16 7PL
www.mobydickgreenlanddock.co.uk
TUBE: Surrey Quays

Morpeth Arms
58 Millbank
Pimlico, SW1P 4RW
TUBE: Pimlico

The Mudlark
4 Montague Close
Southwark, SE1 9DA
TUBE: London Bridge

The Narrow
44 Narrow Street
Limehouse, E14 8DP
www.gordonramsay.com/the-narrow
TUBE: Limehouse (DLR)

The Old Brewery
Pepys Building, Old Royal Naval College
Greenwich, SE10 9LW
www.oldbrewerygreenwich.com
TUBE: Cutty Sark

The Old Ship
25 Upper Mall
Hammersmith, W6 9TD
www.oldshipw6.com
TUBE: Hammersmith

Old Thameside Inn
Pickfords Wharf, Clink Street
London Bridge, SE1 9DG
TUBE: London Bridge

The Palm Tree
Grove Road
Mile End, E3 5BH
TUBE: Mile End

Pepper Saint Ontiod
21 Pepper Street
Millwall, E14 9RP
www.antic-ldt.com/pepper
TUBE: Crossharbour (DLR)

The Pepys
Stew Lane
Mansion House, EC4V 3PT
www.thepepys.co.uk
TUBE: Mansion House

The Pilot Inn
68 River Way
North Greenwich, SE10 0BE
www.pilotgreenwich.co.uk
TUBE: North Greenwich

Pitcher & Piano
11 Bridge Street, Richmond
Surrey, TW9 1TQ
www.pitcherandpiano.com
TRAIN/TUBE: Richmond

Prince of Wales
23 Bridge Road, East Molesey
Surrey, KT8 9EU
www.princeofwaleskt8.co.uk
TRAIN: Hampton Court

Princess of Wales
146 Lea Bridge Road
Clapton, E5 9QB
www.geronimo-inns.co.uk/london-the-princess-of-wales
TUBE: Clapton

The Prospect of Whitby
57 Wapping Wall
Wapping, EW1 3SH
TUBE: Wapping

The Rake
14 Winchester Walk, Borough Market
Southwark, SE1 9AG
TUBE: London Bridge

The Ram
34 High Street, Kingston-upon-Thames
Surrey, KT1 1HL
TRAIN: Kingston-upon-Thames

The Riverside
5 St George's Wharf
Vauxhall, SW8 2LE
www.riversidelondon.com
TUBE: Vauxhall

Rotunda
Kings Place, 90 York Way
King's Cross, N1 9AG
www.rotundabarandrestaurant.co.uk
TUBE: King's Cross St Pancras

The Rutland Ale House
15 Lower Mall
Hammersmith, W6 9DJ
TUBE: Ravenscourt Park

Salt Quay
163 Old Salt Quay
Rotherhithe, SE16 5QU
www.saltquay-rotherhithe.co.uk
TUBE: Rotherhithe

The Ship (Mortlake)
10 Thames Bank
Mortlake, SW14 7QR
TUBE: Kew Gardens

The Ship (Wandsworth)
41 Jews Row
Wandsworth, SW18 1TB
www.theship.co.uk
TUBE: Wandsworth Town

Ship and Whale
2 Gulliver Street
Rotherhithe, SE16 7LT
www.shipandwhale.co.uk
TUBE: Surrey Quays

The Slug and Lettuce
Water Lane, Richmond
Surrey, TW9 1TJ
www.slugandlettuce.co.uk/slug-richmond
TRAIN/TUBE: Richmond

The Swan
50 Manor Road
Walton-on-Thames, KT12 2PF
www.swanwalton.com
TRAIN: Shepperton

Tamesis Dock
Albert Embankment
Vauxhall, SE1 7TP
www.tdock.co.uk
TUBE: Vauxhall

Tide End Cottage
8-10 Ferry Road, Teddington
Middlesex, TW11 9NN
www.tideendcottage-teddington.co.uk
TRAIN: Teddington

Town of Ramsgate
62 Wapping High Street
Wapping, E1W 2PN
www.townoframsgate.co.uk
TUBE: Wapping

Trafalgar Tavern
Park Row
Greenwich, SE10 9NW
www.trafalgartavern.co.uk
TUBE: Cutty Sark

Union Bar and Grill
4 Sheldon Square
Paddington, W2 6EZ
www.theunionbar.co.uk
TUBE: Paddington

Union Tavern
45 Woodfield Road
Maida Vale, W9 2BA
www.union-tavern.co.uk
TUBE: Westbourne Park

The Warwick Castle
6 Warwick Place
Maida Vale, W9 2PX
www.warwickcastlemaidavale.com
TUBE: Warwick Avenue

The Waterfront
Baltimore House, Juniper Drive
Wandsworth, SW18 1TS
www.waterfrontlondon.co.uk
TUBE: Wandsworth Town

Watermans Arms
10-12 Water Lane, Richmond
Surrey, TW9 1TJ
TRAIN/TUBE: Richmond

The Waterside
Riverside Tower, Imperial Wharf
Fulham, SW6 2SU
www.watersideimperialwharf.co.uk
TUBE: Imperial Wharf

The Weir (Brentford)
24 Market Place
Brentford, TW8 8EQ
www.theweirbar.co.uk
TRAIN: Brentford

The Weir (Walton-on-Thames)
Waterside Drive, Walton-on-Thames
Surrey, KT12 2JB
www.weirhotel.co.uk
TRAIN: Walton-on-Thames

The White Cross
Water Lane, Richmond
Surrey, TW9 1TJ
www.thewhitecrossrichmond.com
TRAIN/TUBE: Richmond

The White Swan
Riverside, Twickenham
Middlesex, TW1 3DN
www.whiteswantwickenham.com
TRAIN: Twickenham

The Yacht
5-7 Crane Street
Greenwich, SE10 9NP
TUBE: Cutty Sark

Ye Old Swan
Summer Road, Thames Ditton
Surrey, KT7 0QQ
www.yeoldeswan-thames-ditton.co.uk
TRAIN: Hampton Court

Ye White Hart
Terrace Riverside,
Barnes, SW13 0NR
www.whitehartbarnes.co.uk
TUBE: Barnes Bridge

Photography on jacket, preliminary and end pages features the following pubs:

All photography by Jon Meade unless noted below. All photos used by permission.

Front cover: Trafalgar Tavern (top), The Gun (bottom)
Spine: Cutty Sark Tavern
Back cover: The Market Porter, The Ram, The Ship & Whale
p.1: Cutty Sark Tavern
p.2: The Anglers (Teddington)
p.3: The Bulls Head (Chiswick)
p.5: Trafalgar Tavern
p.6: Cutty Sark Tavern
p.7 (left): Blue Anchor
p.7 (right): Prospect of Whitby
p.8: The Mayflower
p.9: Prospect of Whitby
p.10: Pitcher & Piano
p.11: The Anglers (Teddington)
p.12: The Gazebo
p.13: The Ram
p.14: The Swan (Walton-on-Thames)
p.15: The Boater's Inn
p.16: The Riverside
p.18: The Gipsy Moth
p.19: The Old Brewery
p.20: The Bishop
p.44: Blue Anchor
p.94: Tamesis Dock
p.128: Cutty Sark Tavern
p.156: Prospect of Whitby
p.174: Union Tavern
p.207: The London Apprentice
p.208: The Gazebo

p.7 (top left): Blue Anchor
p.29 (bottom): The Magpie
p.30: Prince of Wales
p.36: The Bishop
p.40: The Ram
p.48 (bottom): The Tide End Cottage
p.51: Barmy Arms
p.52 (bottom): The White Swan
p.66 (top, middle): The City Barge
p.67: The City Barge
p.70 (bottom left): The Ship
p.74, p. 75 (bottom): The Bulls Head (Barnes)
p.81 (top): The Old Ship
p.83: The Dove
p.84 (top): The Rutland Ale House
p. 87 (bottom): Blue Anchor
p.92: The Bricklayer's Arms
p.93 (bottom): The Boathouse
pp.96-97: The Cat's Back
pp.102-103: The Cross Keys
p.104 (bottom left): The Waterside
p.109: Tamesis Dock
p.113: The Pepys
p.114, p. 115: The Banker
p.118 (bottom): The Anchor (Bankside)
p.119 (top): The Market Porter

p.122: The Rake
p.123: The Barrowboy and Banker
pp.136-137: The Mayflower
pp.140-141: Ship and Whale
p.144 (bottom left and right), p. 145: Tim Hampson
p.147 (bottom): The Old Brewery
p.153 (bottom): Cutty Sark Tavern
pp.158-159: Town of Ramsgate
p.163: The Prospect of Whitby
pp.166-167: Tim Hampson
p.168: The Fine Line
p.169: Tim Hampson
p.172 (bottom): The Gun
p.176 (top): The Black Horse
p.178 (bottom), p. 179: The General Eliott
pp.180-181: The Weir (Brentford)
p.184 (top): Tim Hampson
pp.186-187: The Bridge House
p.188 (bottom), p.189: Warwick Castle
p.190: Union Bar and Grill
p.192 (top), p. 193: Tim Hampson
p.196: Rotunda